MICRONESIA: THE GOOD LIFE

The Spiritual Traveler Vol. 2

- A Pictorial Journey -

by p.w. long & Juaquin Santiago

blue ocean press
tokyo

Published by:
blue ocean press, an Imprint of Aoishima Research Institute (ARI)
#807-36 Lions Plaza Ebisu
3-25-3 Higashi, Shibuya-ku
Tokyo, Japan 150-0011
mail@guambooks.com
URL: http://www.guambooks.com

ISBN: 978-4-902837-02-1

"The wisdom is in the basket."
John Mangefel, First Governor of Yap

The wisdom is in the betel nut basket.
Once a difficult problem or conflict arises within
a group of people, it is advisable to stop. Open the
basket and chew the betel nut. Out of this time of
calm, peaceful fellowship in the chewing the nuts
from the basket, clear heads with fresh ideas will
arise, allowing for a collaborative solutions that
benefits all involved. Therefore wisdom us found
in the basket.

This book is dedicated to the late John Mangefel,
a great teacher, statesmen, elder, and son of Micronesia,
whose wisdom can benefit the world as a whole.

Front cover photograph is from a view from a plane flying between Tinian and Saipan

Back cover photograph is of stone money in Yap

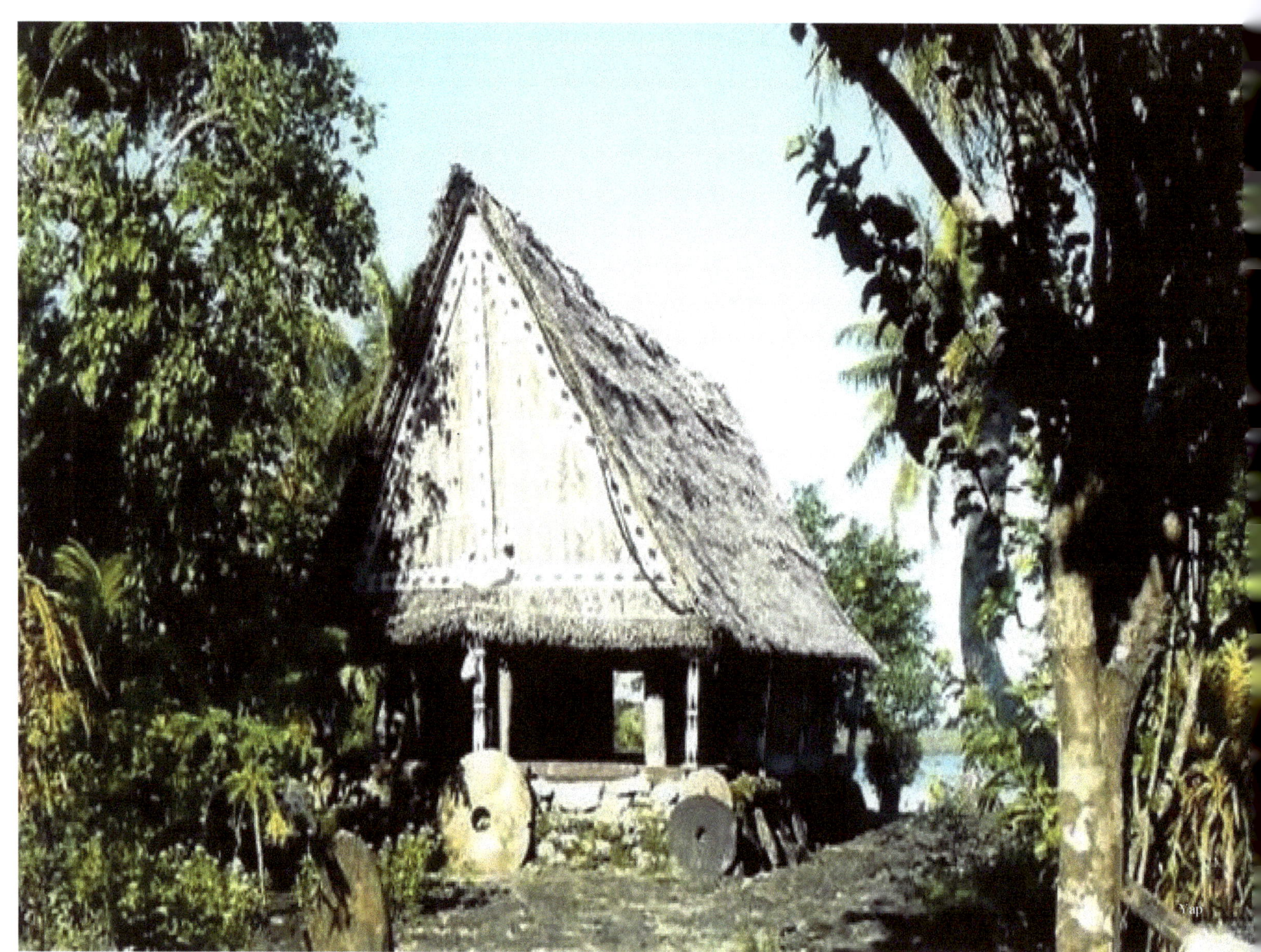
Yap

CONTENTS

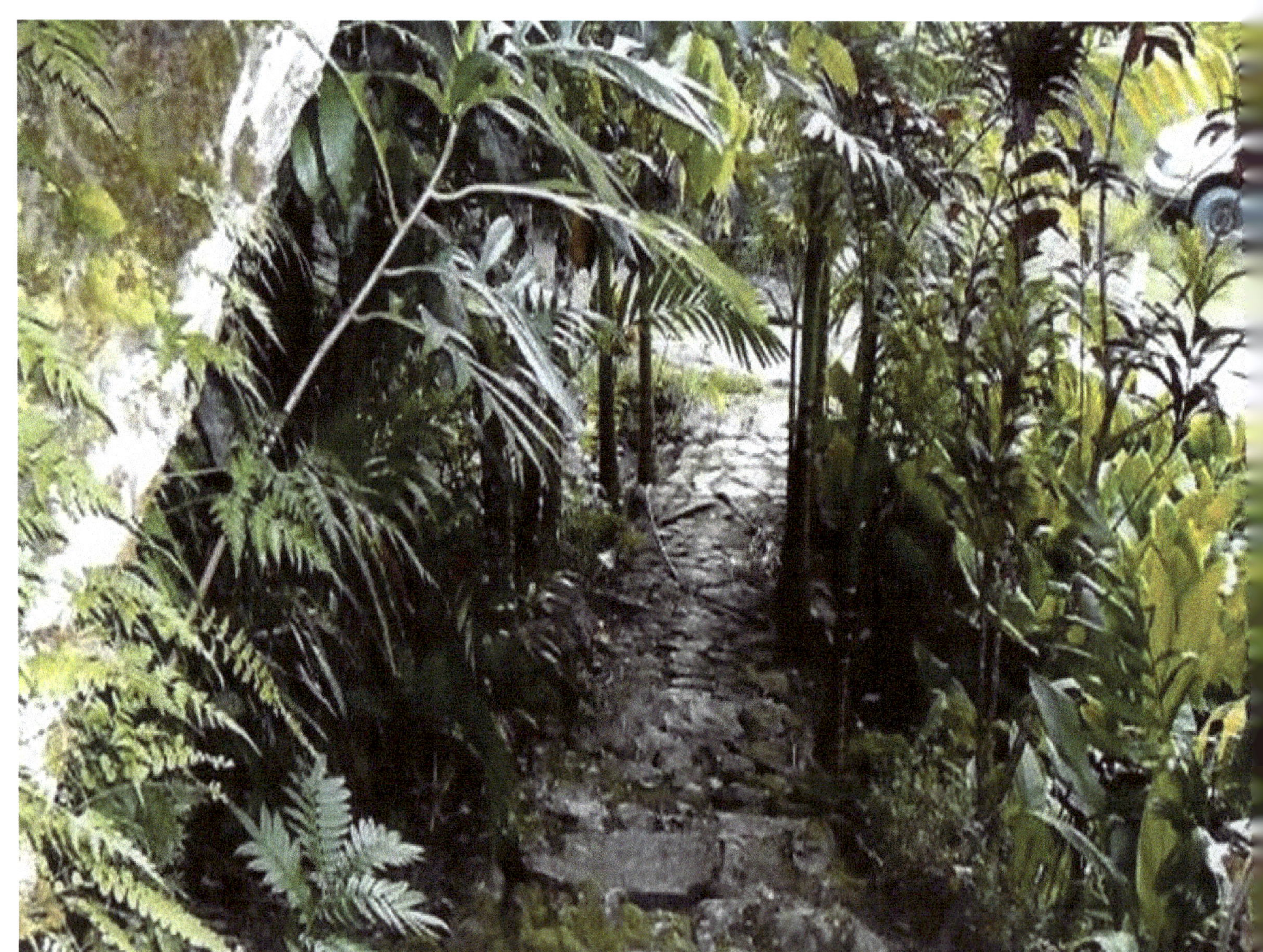

PROLOGUE

The Spiritual Traveler Series:
Instead of simply looking at the sights, sounds, and tastes of a locale,
the reader is allowed to experience the consciousness of a nation.

Travel like all human activities is guided by one's worldview and relationship to the world around them. There is a "default" assumption that travel is a largely consumptive process in which the quality of a travel experience is measured quantitatively, i.e. how many sites seen, how much food eaten, how many shows watched, how many souvenirs purchased, etc. While these do make a strong component of the travel experience, the significant opportunity to develop one's consciousness as a result of one's travel experience can be missed.

Today, human beings are often seen as being disconnected from the environments in which they live, as evidenced in commonly held attitudes that a human presence automatically degrades the natural environment, rather than creating an even more dynamic and sustainable environment than one without humans. Examples of both degradation and dynamism exist where human beings reside; there is no universal "human nature".

As a result of a "consciousness of separation", persons can develop an oppositional rather than integrated relationship between themselves and other persons, and with the natural environment. In the context of travel, persons operating from a "consciousness of separation" are likely to see the persons residing in the locales that they visit as tourists, as essentially "background music", for the experiences that they have while on their vacation.

The aim of this series is to help create a ore holistic travel experience for the reader - to promote The Art of Contemplative Travel™. Contemplative Travel is travel with the intent to develop one's own consciousness as a result of the travel experience. Consciousness is developed through connecting with the people and natural environment around oneself.

Connecting to the people in the locales being traveled to affirms the worldview that develops from living in the realities presented by a particular environment. This enriches the traveler significantly because the traveler experiences the world through the eyes of the people of the locales that they visit. For example, when going to China , have a "Chinese" experience; in Cuba , have a "Cuban" experience; and in Micronesia , have a "Micronesian" experience.

Our diversity as a human family is what makes the world so beautiful; maintaining our diversity is essential to survival as a species as is the case with other organisms in nature.

When the Spiritual Traveler takes you, the reader, to locales in the world, we are introducing a "consciousness theme", the worldview of the residents of that location . Our hope is that when you decide to travel, you will be more inclined to be a "traveler," rather than a tourist, and that you will take advantage of the opportunity to experience life through the eyes of the people whom you are visiting.

Be a Spiritual Traveler by practicing the Art of Contemplative Travel™

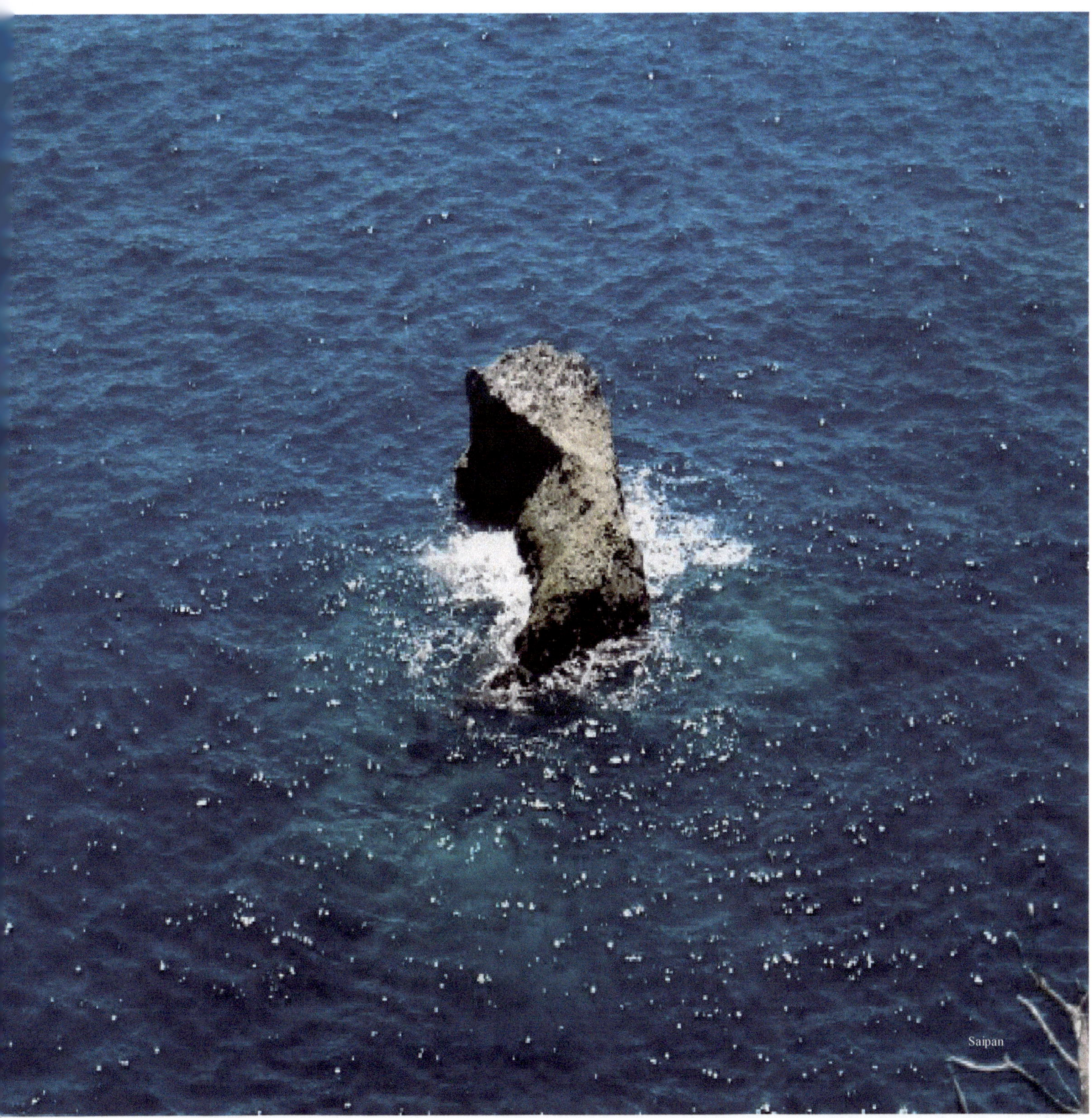
Saipan

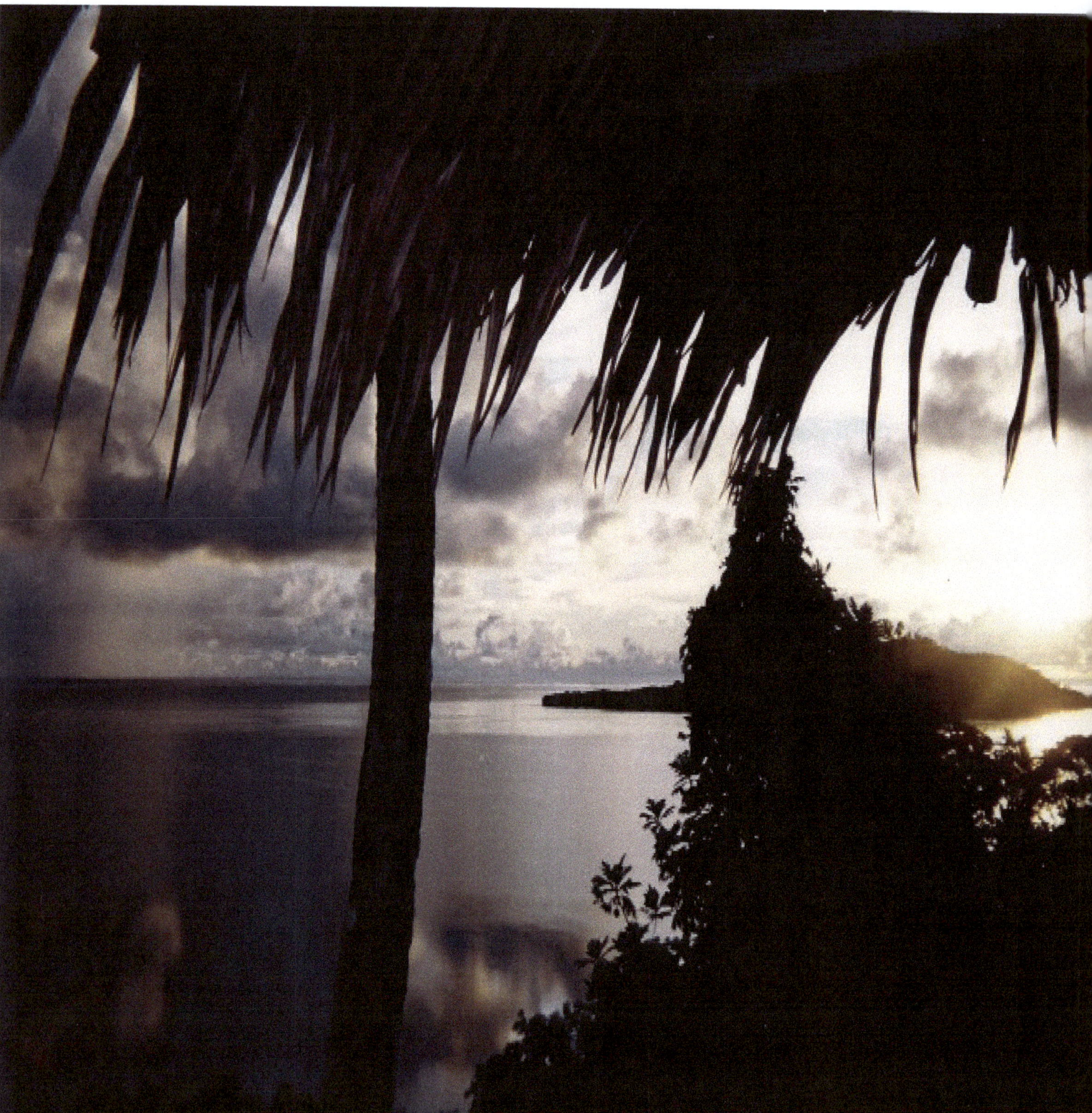

INTRODUCTION: THE GOOD LIFE

I am just weeks returning from Micronesia, as I begin this book of essays. I find myself ensconced in the perfect setting, right smack in the middle of the good life itself, here on Marco Island, Florida (part of the "Paradise Coast") as I begin the ponder the meaning of the "good life".

The Calusa Indians must have been seeking the good life when they first came to this island from the Mayan region of South America. Known as one of the shelling capitals of Florida, tourists descend upon the Calusa shell mounds that remain. It is said that the Calusa's collected and formed mounds of shells for ancient religious ceremonies and for protection against the tidal surge of hurricanes. Now the shells serve a much more mundane purpose; depending upon the quantity that you can find to take home, they are an indicator of the good life that one has enjoyed while visiting the island.

The Island's tourist guide exhorts you to consider Marco Island, "your personal playground". This is an island of white-sand beaches, surrounded by Gulf Waters that boast the best fishing in the state. The island reeks of the "good life", it is EVERYWHERE. There are exquisite waterfront homes, elegant high-rises, and gated golf communities. But mostly, there are what everyone who partakes of the good life expects, plenty of things to buy. The island is a consumer's heaven. Here, Tommy Bahama resort wear competes with exquisite island wear, exotic swimwear, and of course, designer fashions. There is fine dining, fine jewelry, and fine artwork. Even animals on Marco Island enjoy the good life. They are treated to "doggie grooming", a doggie boutique, and a doggie daycare. How much better can the good life be? Even for pets.

As I began to write, I was distracted by a nearby conversation. To be sure, I am no eavesdropper, when I want information I conduct interviews, but this was interesting. Two couples, sitting by the pool, enjoying the good life, were of all things talking about crime and violence in the

United States. Drive-by shootings, innocent victims, little girls being snatched from their beds as they slept, and cars being stolen right from in front of houses has driven at least one of the couples to have four dogs for protection. At this point, I am wondering if perhaps the good life only really exists at resorts on islands such as this, for a seven-day stay but I continue to listen. The conversation moves to the changing neighborhoods (my ears really perk up). Now what used to be "good neighborhoods" (where middle-class people are supposed to enjoy the good life) are being taken over by immigrants, "without green cards" and folks whose rent is being subsidized with government" Section 8" vouchers." Is the good life about to end?" The conversation finishes on a somber note;" the children from dysfunctional relationships," and yes there is even admittedly some dysfunction in their own families. By now, I am beginning to doubt if there is such a thing as the "good life". But before I become too cynical, I come back to myself and remember why I am here in the first place.

This environment, surrounded by luxury yachts and magnificent homes, actually serves my purpose very well. It is worlds away from whence I have just returned; and the contrasts are so great that it presents the ideal setting to really understand what makes one's life good. Is it an abundance of luxury items? Is it being able to live in mammoth house, to drive the largest car on the road? Is it being able to wear the most expensive clothes? Is it being able to afford to spend a week at an island resort? Or is it something far less complicated? Is the good life freedom from lack or the sense of lack? Is it freedom from fear? Is it being able to instantly partake of nature's beauty and bounty? Is it simple peace of mind?

The smooth sound of Wes Montgomery's *Bumpin on Sunset*, floats on the breeze from a nearby bar, and I am reminded of looking out upon the lagoon from the Tide Table Bar at the Robert Reimers Hotel in Majuro. Sipping a glass of Cabernet Sauvignon, and nodding to the beat of Wes, I believe that for the next few days, as I reflect upon my stay in Micronesia, I will somehow come to understand the true meaning of the good life.

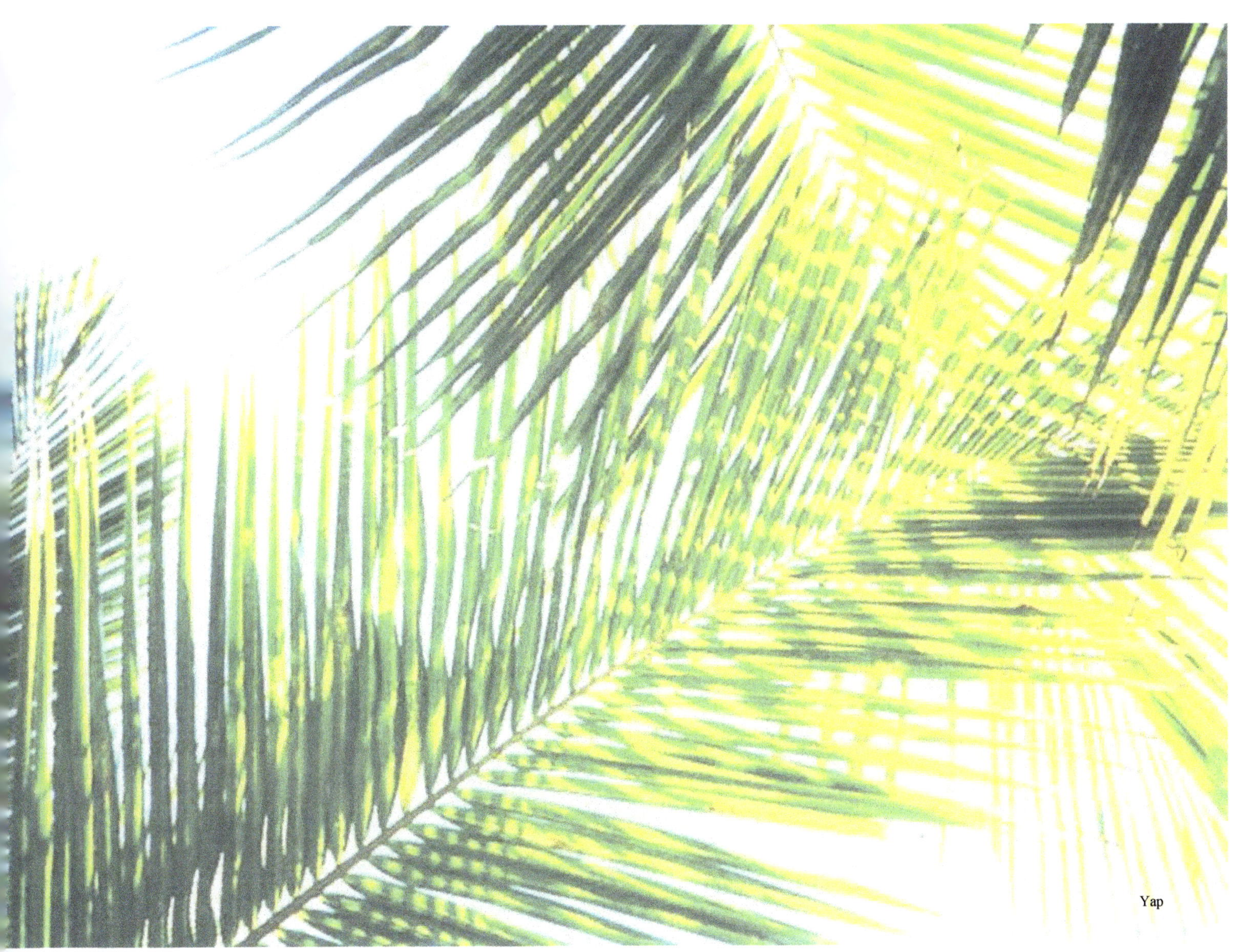

Yap

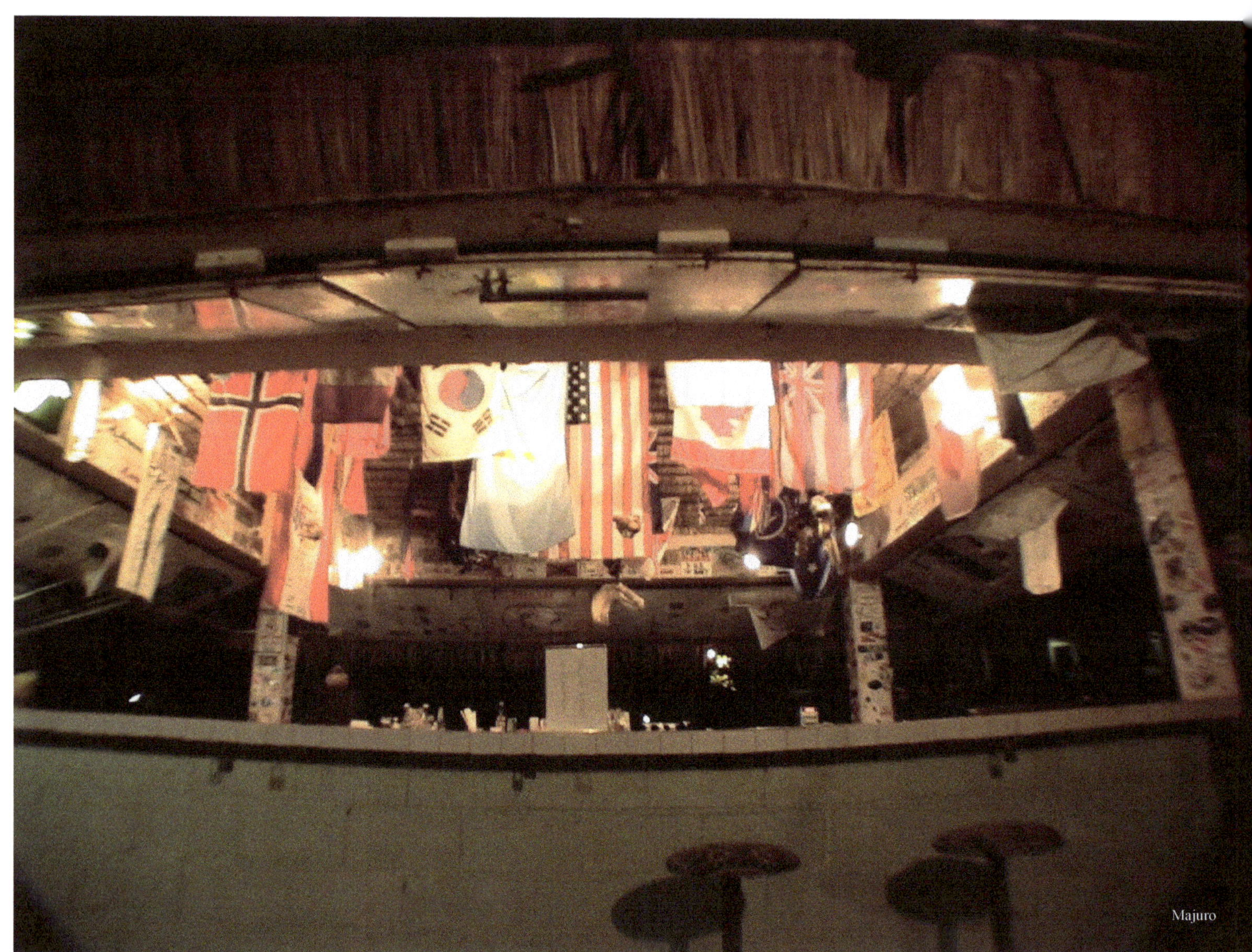

Majuro

MAJURO ARRIVAL

My four o'clock awakening to catch the 7:30 flight from Honolulu to Majuro dulled my senses to the point that I had no will left to conjure up expectations or even excitement about my arrival on the "Pearl of the Pacific". So I completely surrendered to the experience. I had no idea (except for maybe my readings upon which my mind could not now register) of what was in store for me. There were no preconceived notions and no prior experience to which I could connect.

Deplaning, I felt the initial disorientation that I often feel when I enter an entirely new environment. A little anxiety set in as I tried to get my bearings. "Not so fast, take it easy, let it all in", I told myself, "you've got time, eight days to be exact". After gathering my luggage and going through customs, I entered a new world which was initially curiously reminiscent of an earlier one that I had known. A choir singing strands of what sounded very much like old southern Black spirituals greeted us. It was strangely familiar, the same cadence; like the old women "lining a hymn" that I had heard so often as a child.

We made our way through the maze of brown-skinned, high-cheekboned women who greeted us and placed wreaths of flowers on our heads to the Robert Reimers Hotel van.

We begin our journey to the good life on what has been called the "longest and best drive in Micronesia". The airport is 12 miles from the DUP municipality, which is compromises three towns, Delap, Uliga, and Darrit , better known as Rita, which is where most of the main services and sights are located. Being southern myself, all of this feels like some small southern town cast upon an island years earlier. We pass "real" people who live close to the earth, even prefer to sleep out there on the cool ground or on cars outside. I see people who may not have all of the "material comforts" but who possess a joy of spirit that is readily evident. I know immediately that I like these people. It feels very comfortable here. Our drive on this narrow stretch of highway takes us past shanties, cement houses and houses made of steel containers. We passed groups of children playing, men gathered talking, and women sweeping coral rock yards. Dogs were napping, pigs rooted coconuts, and the family wash hung drying on bushes in the yard near family burial plots. On our way were small neighborhood stores selling staples, sweets, and betel nuts, as well as the Copra plant, government buildings, and the new Marshall Islands Resort. The ocean can be seen on both sides of this ribbon of land and in the near distance we spot Chinese trawlers fishing for and processing tuna.

When we finally reach the Robert Reimers Hotel, which is located on the 2nd floor of the RRE Professional Building, the scene is almost surreal; the street below has the look and feel of some dusty Texas town in the 1900's. I settle in upstairs and begin my exploration of the good life.

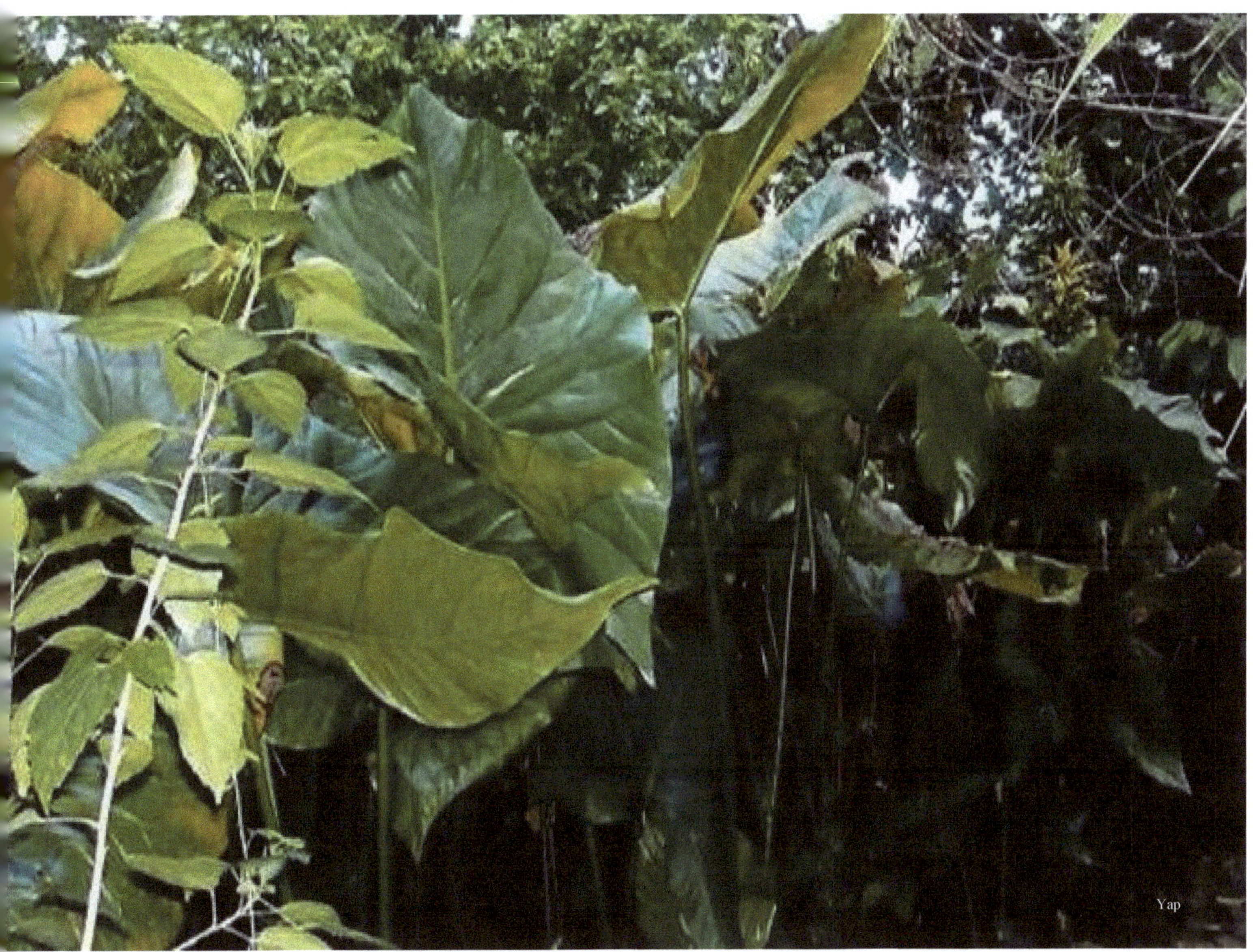

Yap

Palau

THE GOOD LIFE

A sense of lack in our physical and emotional worlds is a pervasive and powerful motivating force that keeps us on edge, craving more and more. Most of us in the Western world struggle with this demon and are slaves to the needs and desires that this sense of lack creates. We are constantly attempting to acquire more of something or something bigger and better than what we already have. No matter how "well" we live, we are continuously striving to attain more because the sense of lack pervades our consciousness. When we truly live the "good life", we are free from the sense of lack; our physical, emotional, and spiritual needs are met.

Micronesia, especially its culturally isolated islands might easily be considered to be paradise, for it is here that truly the "good life" exists. Life on these islands lived close to nature, in conjunction with the land and sea, is not a struggle. There is no sense of lack; everything needed for one's physical, emotional, and spiritual well-being is provided either by nature or the culture. Hunger and famine are not concepts known to these islanders as nature provides a bountiful supply of staple foods, which provide both sustenance and adequate nutrition. Taro (and its green leaves), yams, sweet potatoes, breadfruit, and coconuts provide the necessary carbohydrates and fat in the diet, while fish, crabs, chicken, and pigs supply the needed protein.

The coconut palm, the most important plant on the islands, might easily be considered a "miracle" plant. This tree alone not only provides food, drink, fuel, shelter, natural good, but economic revenue as well. The islanders use the green coconut husks to make rope, while fuel and charcoal are made from the mature husks. The wood of the tree is used for lumber and carvings, while the fronds are utilized as thatch for roofs and for weaving baskets. Copra or the dried meat of the nut is the source of coconut oil, the region's principal export and main source of revenue for the out islands. Other trees; breadfruit, tropical mahogany, betel nut, and the pandanus are also a source of materials to provide shelter and for making material goods such as mats, baskets, and fans.

The sense of safety and security that increasingly eludes us in the West is an ever-present force in the life of these islanders. One neighbor-islander explained that "there is no fear". Doors are left unlocked, and it is customary for islanders to sleep outside on a mattress. Even in the more urban Majuro, when the traveler took her morning walk at 6:30 AM, a common sight was people sleeping outside with no apparent fear of being harmed. The question must be asked: "Is one truly living the good life when he or she lives with the constant fear that he or she will be harmed or their possessions taken?

Micronesian societies are some of the most collectivistic in the world with the most highly communal lifestyles. Extended families are the norm with grandparents, married children, and adopted kin living under the same roof. Shared food, resources, work, and play are all that they know. Whether it is fishing, working in taro patches, or collecting copra, it is a group effort with all persons in the group benefiting. Individualism is taboo; the person who only "looks out for number one" and who is considered to be "selfish", stands out in this society. As a result, he or she is "left out". The islanders say that selfish people "don't last long" and "will eventually change".

The sense of alienation, isolation, and separateness that individualism produces is non-existent. The psychological need that all human beings have for belonging is met through the islanders' collectivistic culture. There is simply no sense of separateness; one is defined by being a part of a family, clan, and village. One's sense of esteem is derived from being part of the collective. Although some highly-stratified caste hierarchies with chiefs, royalty, and the like are part of the cultural context, these do not cause the psychic damage similar to that experienced by minorities in the West. Everyone in the group has some value and worth as a person; there is not concept of superior or inferior beings.

   It is in fact this set of collectivistic values that bind families, clans, and villages that contributes to the quality of life and well-being that the islanders enjoy. Sharing of food (there are no hungry); shelter (there are no homeless) and work is the norm for these island societies. Respect for elders, respect for tradition, observing customs related to death, and transfer of group knowledge through the grandparents and community service are strongly held values. It is through these collectivistic values that the islanders gain a sense of happiness, freedom, and even personal power.

Life on these islands is simple with lush vegetation, warm tranquil waters, pristine beaches, and the world's most uniform (80 degrees F) temperatures. Traditional Micronesian life is steeped in colorful traditions and guided by a set of beliefs, values, and norms which promote the well-being of all its members. So what is the good life really? Perhaps these islanders know the secret: taking just enough from nature to adequately feed their bodies, while connecting enough with each other and the earth to feel their spirits.

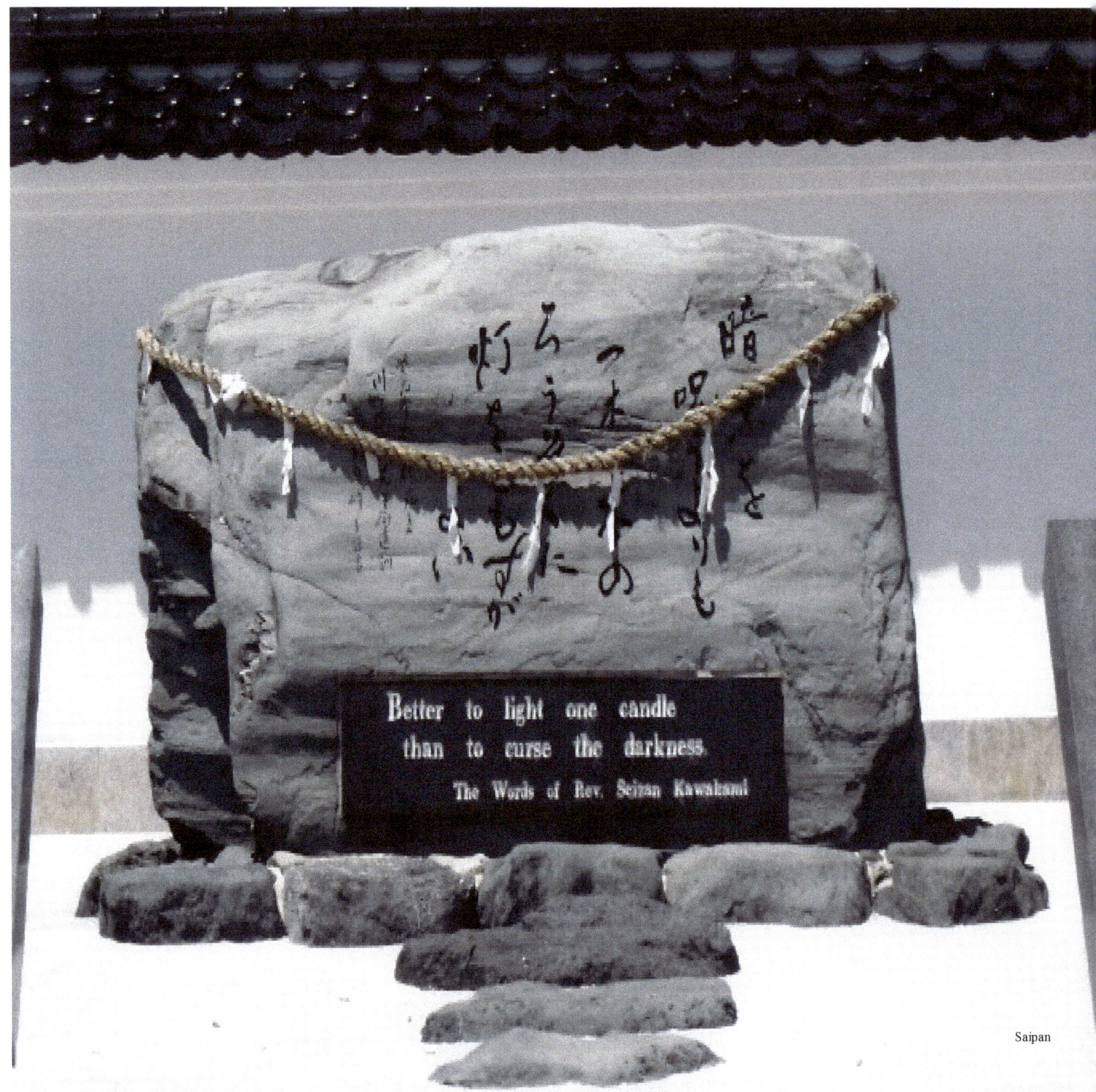
Better to light one candle
than to curse the darkness.
The Words of Rev. Seizan Kawakami

Saipan

BUT ALL IS NOT PRETTY AND PRISTINE

The Rongelap Atoll is one of the 29 atolls and five islands in the Central Pacific region that make up the Republic of the Marshall Islands (RMI). Sixty-one islets with a combined area of approximately three square mile make up the land area of the atoll and the lagoon coves some 388 square miles. Rongelap Atoll is advertised as "pristine and uninhabited, but big fish and clear water". In fact, Rongelap Atoll and the surrounding islands are said to be home to possibly the most pristine waters in the world. But all is not pretty and pristine, you have only to visit the Alele Museum in Majuro to see the sad and ugly history of the Rongelapese people.

The Alele Museum is all of one large room housed on the top floor adjacent to the library in a two-story building next to the courthouse. This small museum contains exhibits of early Marshallese culture, including stick charts, model canoes, and other artifacts. Most poignant however, are the stark black and white photographs of Rongelapese villagers taken after the bomb test of 1954. The degree of man's inhumanity toward other men is evident in these photographs.

On March 1, 1954, the idyllic life of the Rongelapese people changed forever, and the people who lived there would never know the good life again. The Rongelapese became unwilling participants in the nuclear history archives when the U.S. conducted a nuclear test code-named Bravo in the northern Marshall Islands. The immensely powerful blast sent clouds of deadly radioactive dust toward the inhabited Rongelap Atoll, some 100 miles to the east. The fallout came as powdered ash some 3-6 hours after the blast. As a two inch layer of radioactive ash formed on the island, the drinking water turned a brackish yellow, and children played in the fallout. By nightfall, the Rongelapese became terrified as their hair began to fall out and they experience severe vomiting and diarrhea. After three days, and too late to help many, the villagers were relocated to Kwajalein for medical treatment and then moved to Ejit Island on Majuro Atoll.

The Rongelap community spent the next three years living on Ejit Island before returning home to Rongelap in June, 1957. Because of growing concerns about contamination the islanders were evacuated a second time by the Greenpeace ship, Rainbow Warrior to a new temporary home on Mejalto Island on Kwajalein Atoll in 1985. In 1995, the U.S. established a $45 million trust fund for the Rongelapese and the rehabilitation of the island began soon after.

As the photographs in the Alele Museum attest, the Rongelapese have continuing health problems as a result of the contamination that include mental retardation, leukemia, stillbirths, and miscarriages. Almost 75 percent of the people who were under the age of ten on the day of the blast had had surgery for thyroid tumors.

Testimony by atomic energy officials revealed that the day before the bomb test, U.S. meteorologists reported that the winds had shifted in the direction of Rongelap and a warning had been issued that contamination of the islands would occur. The Rongelapese received no warnings from the U.S. government about the testing or its potential effects. In fact, it has been said that a decision was made to go forward with the tests despite knowledge that the winds were blowing in the direction of inhabited atolls. This unconscionable decision was essentially a choice to irradiate the Rongelapese people. The goal of the Rongelapese people is to be able to return one day to their ancestral homeland, however, the Rongelapese will never be able to return to the good life that they once knew.

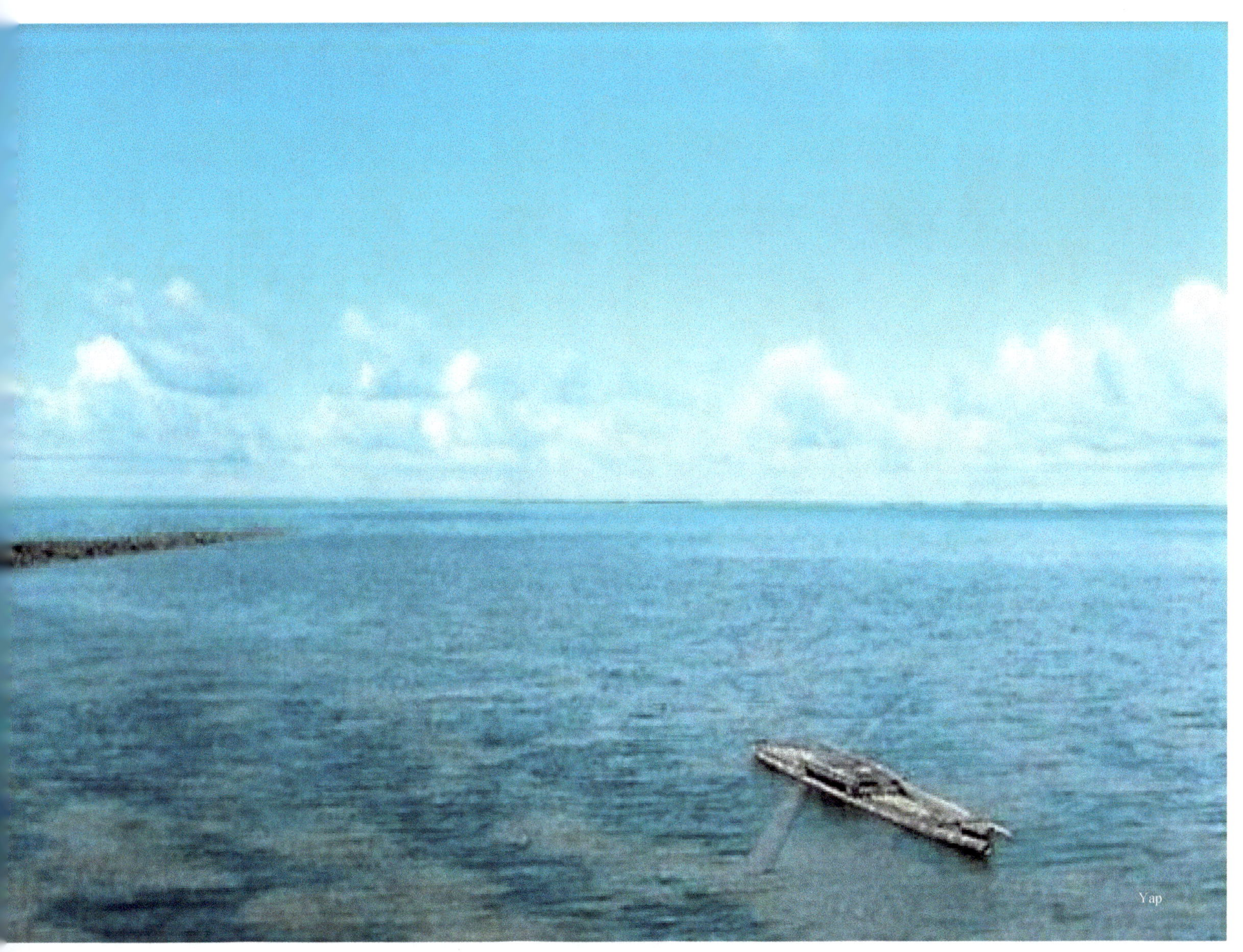

Yap

Tunian - - Saipan

A TALE OF TWO ISLANDS

My view of Kwajalein or "Kwaj" as it is called, was strictly from the window of a Continental jet enroute from Honolulu, which I boarded in Majuro. Except for those deplaning (U.S. military and contract workers), the rest of us, mostly brown people sat on the plane as it was searched (for ?????), and given permission to take-off for Pohnpei. When I decided to get a better view of the island from the door of the plane, I was abruptly and in some seriously threatening tones told to go back to my seat from someone on a loudspeaker in the terminal. "Kwaj" is strictly off-limits to unofficial visitors except as a transit point to neighboring Ebeye. In order to stay overnight on Kwaj, one must have an official sponsor on the island.

Kwajalein Atoll, some 2100 nautical miles west of Honolulu, is part of the Republic of the Marshall Islands (RMI). It is the world's largest coral atoll and surrounds the world's largest lagoon. Most significantly, it is home to a U.S. $4 billion space tracking and missile defense facility. The lagoon is the target and splashdown point for U.S. intercontinental ballistic missiles (ICBM's) fired from Vandenburg Air Force Base in California, some 4000 miles away. Eleven of the islands comprising Kwajalein Atoll are leased by the U.S. from the RMI government to accommodate the Ronald Reagan Ballistic Defense Test Site or RTS. "Kwaj" is a world of radar installations, optic sensors, telemetry, huge antennae, and sophisticated communications equipment used for ballistic missile, missile interceptor, and space operations support.

Approximately 2700 U.S. civilian contract workers and their families live in what can be considered "Micronesia's gated community". From what one is able to see from the airplane window, "Kwaj" is a well-kept, beautifully manicured tropical environment. It is in fact an U.S. suburb in Micronesia. Housing on the island ranges from single rooms in BQ's (bachelor quarters) to trailers, older concrete houses, newer wooden houses, townhouses and three-bedroom, two-bath energy efficient dome houses resistant to weather damage.

There is a fully accredited school system consisting of an elementary and junior/senior high school. Neither adults nor children should suffer from boredom on the island as there are an abundance of recreational facilities and activities. There is a golf course (from the window of the airplane you can see them playing a round), two swimming pools, tennis courts, two cinemas (one outdoor), fitness centers, a skate park, and a bowling alley. If that isn't enough to keep the residents occupied, there are all the pleasures of a first-rate resort available: scuba diving, deep sea fishing, windsurfing, and kayaking. There is a "Surfway" grocery store, Macy's and Macy's West, video rentals, and a convenience store, as well as a bank, restaurant, laundry/dry cleaners, barber shop, beauty salon, travel agency, two bars, and a club at the golf course, just like home. What is there to miss?

Some three miles to the north of Kwajalein is Ebeye, known as the "slum of the Pacific". Over 1300 Marshallese laborers who work on Kwajalein and support close to 12,000 more relatives and friends, live in inadequate, overcrowded tenement conditions on an island (1.6 km) one mile long and less than 200 yards (183 m) wide.

When the missile range was developed in the 1960's, Kwajalein island residents were evacuated to Ebeye, as well as the residents of many other islands to free up most of the lagoon for catching missiles launched from California. Menial jobs on the base then attracted Marshallese from other atolls.

The contrasts between Kwajalein and Ebeye are startling. On Ebeye's 78-acres, one of the most densely populated areas in the world there is no room for trees. Ebeye's residents live on top of each other in one-room shacks and lean-to's made of plywood, tin, cinder block, and plastic sheeting. Sanitation conditions are appalling; a new sewage system built in 1979 broke down soon after its completion and pollution levels are 100 times higher than are those considered safe by the World Health Organization. Typhoid and dysentery were once in epidemic proportions. Ebeye's electrical power is out more often than not, and running water is often restricted to as little as 15 minutes a day.

It is ironic however, that even though Kwajalein is owned by and leased to the U.S. by the Marshallese, they cannot sleep on Kwajalein. Neither are Marshallese allowed to shop at the subsidized stores or swim in the public pools. Marshallese workers are shuttled by boat between their barely livable conditions on Ebeye to their affluent work sites on Kwajalein. At best, they are issued day passes to do laundry and to haul sanitary drinking water back to Kwajalein. This is Micronesia's brand of apartheid.

During the 1960's, the usually passive Marshallese disrupted military tests by staging a series of "sail-ins" to restricted parts of the atoll. This action was the impetus for renegotiating the lease agreement between the U.S. and the Marshallese. The rent was increased from approximately $200,000 to U.S. $9 million a year. Half of the money was allotted to development and the Kwajalein Atoll Development Authority was established. Since then, some minor improvements have occurred on Ebeye; the sewage system has been rebuilt, sidewalks built, and potholed roads repaired. Ebeye still, however, when compared to the other island, "Kwaj", is reminiscent of the segregated south of the 1950's.

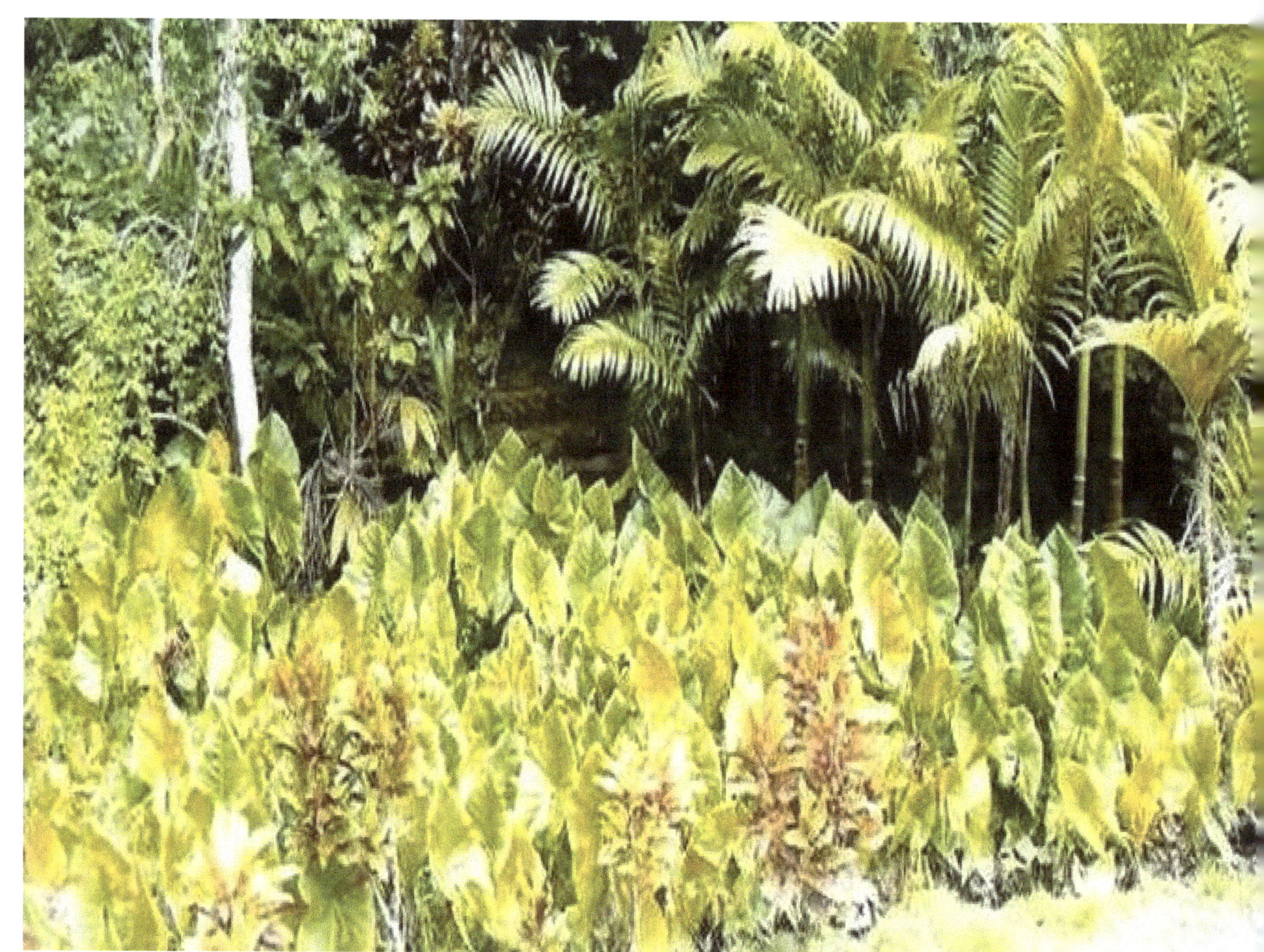

EATING THEMSELVES TO DEATH

Food psychologists, if there is such a professional would surely tell us that the food we eat does more than fill our stomachs; it fulfills our emotional needs as well. The type of food that we eat is both an indicator of our economic and social status. Ultimately being able to eat or not eat certain foods can elevate or lessen our esteem. What we can or cannot eat influences our feelings about whether or not we are partaking of the good life.

Our status is inherent in the foods we eat. As working class people move into the middle class, their diet changes. Not always because they enjoy the higher status food more but because they are supposed to. They forsake beans and greens for steak and chops. They would be embarrassed beyond words to let anyone know that in years past, they had made meals of sardines or pork and beans. When one has "arrived", one eats like it.

Historically, Micronesian cultures had eaten a traditional diet. A traditional diet being one which the culture had followed for centuries prior to the industrial revolution. For Micronesians, part of the good life was an abundance of foods that provided the perfect combination of carbohydrates, fats, and proteins. These staple foods were taro, breadfruit, greens from the taro plant, bananas, fish, limited chicken or wild pig for celebrations. All of these foods were eaten in their natural state; not processed, meaning no added white flour, sugar, or salt. These foods were either steamed, boiled, baked, or roasted, never fried. The eating habits of the healthiest cultures consisted of large volumes of unrefined carbohydrates, moderate amounts of protein, mostly from vegetable sources, and a few fats. After World War II, when an U.S. Navy team surveyed the health of the islanders, they found an absence of malnutrition and obesity, and there was no evidence of diabetes or hypertension.

An influx of U.S. dollars and the change to the money economy changed the way Micronesians perception of food, and had a significant impact on their diets. With government jobs and dollars to spend, Micronesians began to eat imported and processed foods. "Arriving" came to mean having the dollars to spend to buy rice, spam, ketchup, soy sauce, and lots of foods filled with sugar. Those capable of purchasing these new Western foods moved into the higher status than those who traditionally cultivated, caught, or prepared the food. More critically, Micronesians are guided by some vague mistaken notion that processed food is superior to the traditional foods, and as a result are literally eating themselves to death.

Especially in the more urban areas, a trip to the grocery store is exceedingly painful, as one wants to empty shopping carts and ask the customers "what on earth are you doing?" Shopping carts are filled to the brim with every imaginable and available product made with white flour, sugar, and salt. Cans of spam, packages of turkey tails (yuk!), and rice compete with chips, sodas, and all varieties of Little Debbie cakes. As they partake of these fatty and processed foods, these once healthy people are introduced to poisonous chemicals, artificial growth hormones, and unregulated antibiotics.

The outcome of the new "affluent" lifestyle in Micronesia was the rise of health hazards associated with "modernization". As the Micronesian diet changed, new nutritional problems and subsequent diet-related illnesses occurred. Micronesians are succumbing to heart disease, cancer, strokes, and the pervasive obesity and diabetes in epidemic proportions.

To make mattes worse, dependence on Western foods is increasing. The typical dinner has become spam and rice covered with soy sauce or ketchup, and when Micronesians are not able to get these foods, they experience a "psychological" hunger that traditional foods can no long satisfy. These imported foods have a higher fat, sugar, and salt content than traditional foods resulting in more obesity, hypertension, heart disease, and diabetes. "Sugar sickness" is one of the major health problems in the islands. Eighty percent of the populace of The Federated States of Micronesia is obese; 35 percent suffer from hypertension; and 20-50 percent of the population is affected by diabetes.

What is so ironic is that the traditional, now perceived to be "lower status" foods are so much more healthy and nutritious. As Micronesians seek to experience the good life through the foods that they eat, they are giving up what they seek. The good life is in actuality one that is healthy; a life free from chronic pain, disease, and illness. The chronic diseases that plague present-day Micronesians were rare among their ancestors. Healthy cultures eat traditional food. Perhaps, one day before it is too late for too many generations, present-day Micronesians will return to the wisdom of their ancestors and again enjoy the good life.

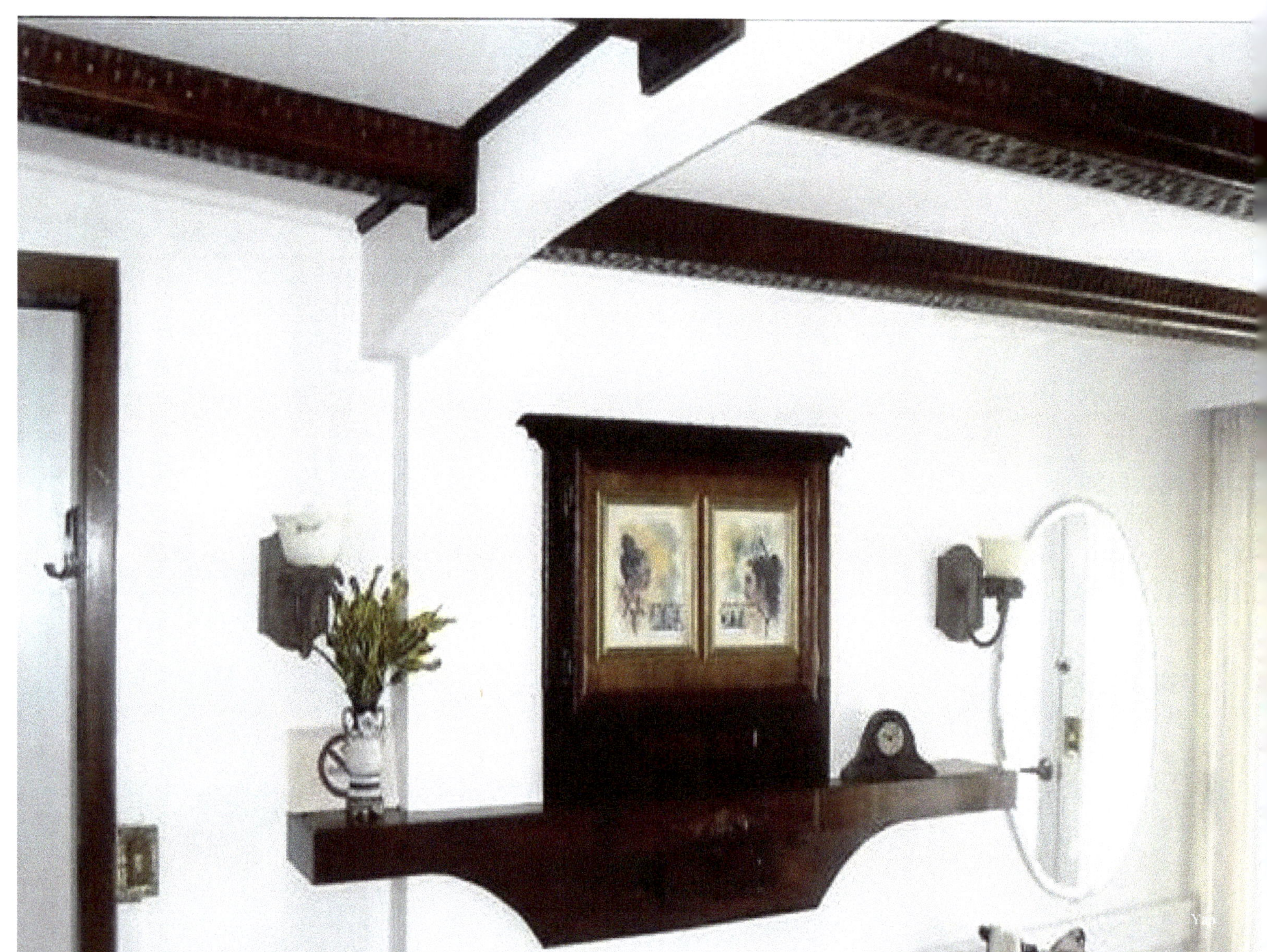

LEAVING MAJURO

Leaving Majuro turned out to be infinitely more difficult than the arrival. We were advised by the hotel staff to arrive at the airport some four hours before the flight. They vaguely mentioned something about standing in line but in no way prepared us for the frustrating experience that was to come. When we arrived to our utter surprise, we were told that the flight was overbooked and that our seats had been given away. With what seemed like at least twenty other frustrated travelers, we sat in the tiny coffee shop and waited for "our boarding passes to be released". Maybe I should say, we waited to see if we were going to get a boarding pass at all or wait for three days to get the next flight out.

For those who travel this route often, this was just part of the process of trying to leave Majuro. It seems that passengers on the leg of the flight from Majuro to Kwajalein are frequently bumped to make room for contract workers traveling to Kwajalein from Honolulu (who evidently have priority status).

I have managed to chalk that experience up as just another of "life's lessons", this lesson being "patience". When I inquired on one gentleman who had been in line with me, as to how he was able to get a boarding pass, he simply replied "patience". Maybe I learned something that day not only about the island way of doing things but that the Serenity Prayer really does work. Initially, I had demanded to see the airline manager (you know the usual way we deal with inconveniences in the U.S.). I of course used my polite albeit assertiveness training to inform her that we did have the paperwork to prove that our seats were already assigned. But after being assertive in the islands, all one is left with is patience. So I patiently detached from the whole idea of even being able to leave Majuro on that particular flight or day. Instead, I planned all of the things that I would do if I had three more days to spend in Majuro. I detached from the belief that our itinerary would be "messed up". Luckily, or by the grace of God, we did get boarding passes and departed as scheduled. I was hot, wet, tired, and weary, but proud of my ability to detach and go with the Micronesian flow.

I would not let that little experience ruin my memories of those eight days in paradise. Being awakened by crowing roosters, smelling the fragrant vegetation below my balcony, watching sailboats in the lagoon, all of this was very special. I especially enjoying our morning walks before Majuro woke up. We walked each day at around 6:30; some of the workers at the hotel told us to be careful of dogs, however. "These are mean dogs here", they warned, " if they come toward you, get down and throw a stone". Well, being true to the way in which we had been socialized in the U.S. to deal with danger, we got a weapon, a stick in fact. As it turned out, we did not need our sticks as even the dogs in Majuro sleep late; they were never awake when we took our walk. Life is easy here.

The most impressive aspect of the stay at the Robert Reimers was the daily visit to the Tide Table Restaurant by the "Irooj" or chief. He was one rather handsome, immaculately dressed, wearing a little understated "bling", classy, elderly gentleman. Each day he presided over the Tide Table in a very "chiefly" manner. He was usually there each day for breakfast, and stayed until well into the afternoon greeting his "subjects" and often talking with small groups of children who were brought to see him. He seemed to be the model of how to live in the two worlds of which Micronesia is now a part. He was modern, had and used his cell phone and obviously enjoyed the advantages that the rental of Kwajalein provided, but he was also very authentic. He maintained his cultural essence; he was a joy to watch. Perhaps the greatest lesson learned in Majuro about the "good life" if that one can only experience and enjoy it as a whole, authentic person, remaining true to one's cultural center; anything less than that is probably only the illusion of the good life.

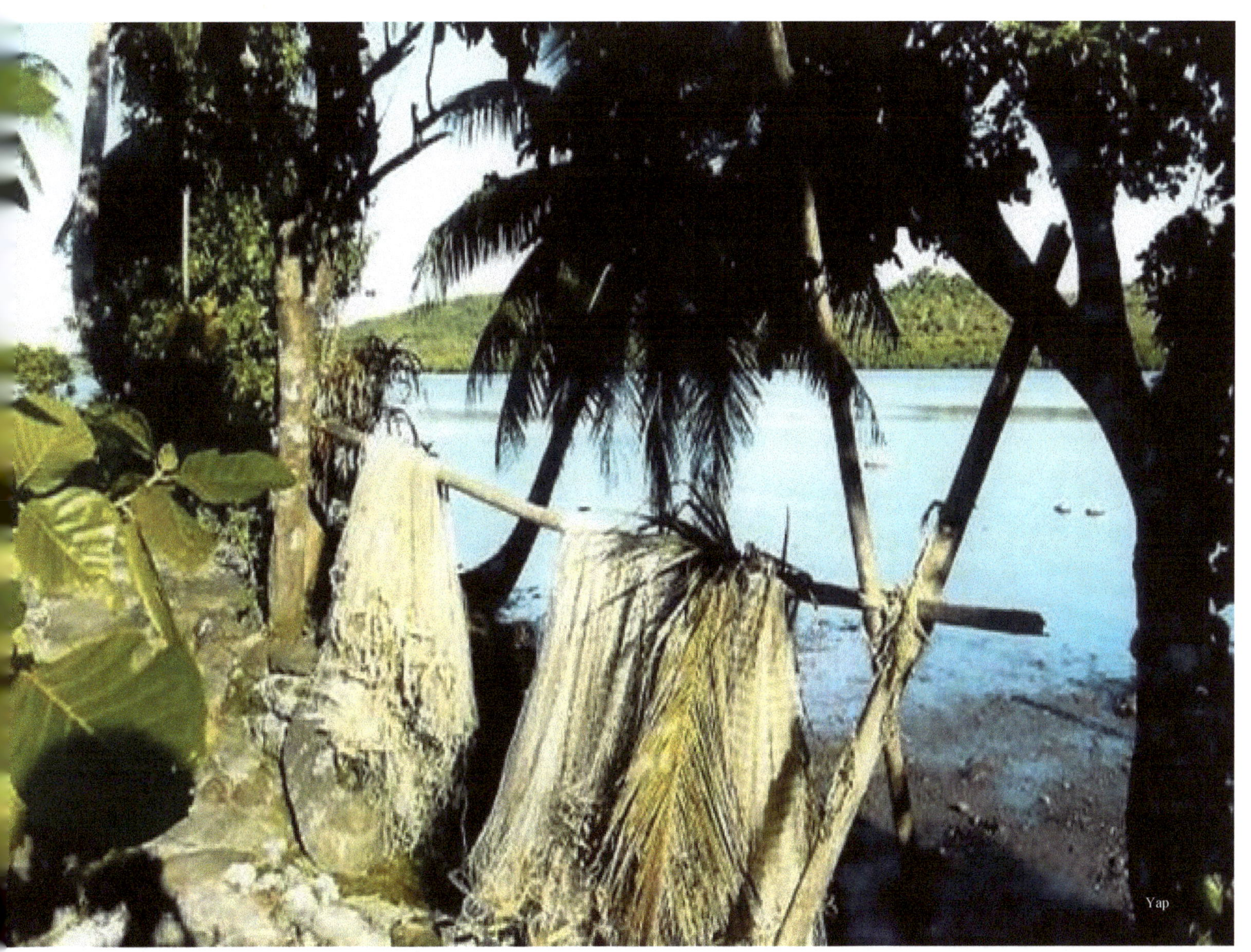

Yap

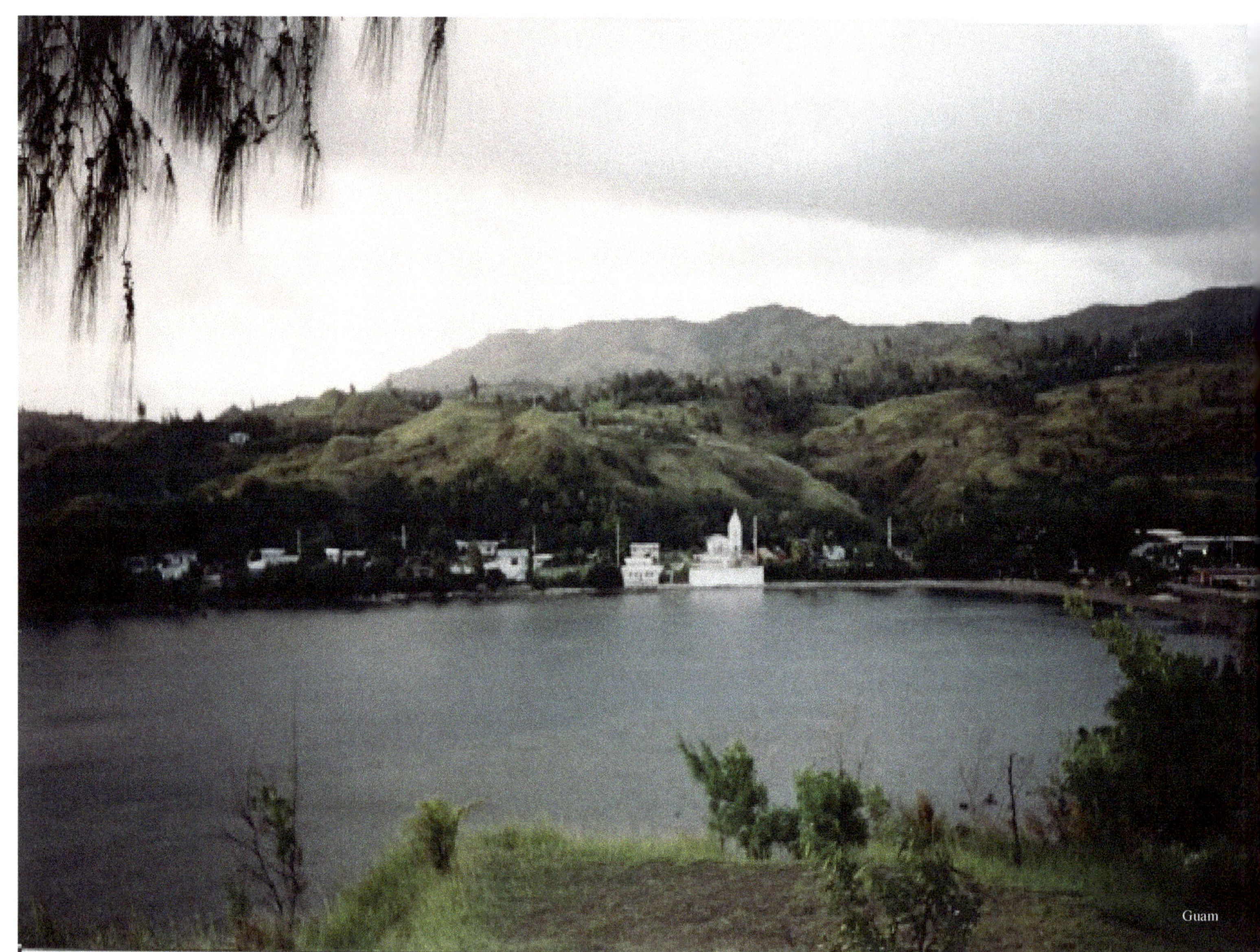

Guam

A MOST RESILIENT PEOPLE

The first time I sat foot on Guam (*Guahan* in the indigenous Chamorro language), I was overwhelmed by a pervasive sense of emptiness. It seemed to be lifeless, a landscape devoid of character or spirit. With all of its fast food joints and gas stations, it reminded me of some southwestern town in the United States that had been dropped on some Pacific island. Upon first sight, one would never believe that this was the home of a people who have lived on this island for thousands of years.

The *traveler* has made five trips to Guam, and with each trip, she goes a little deeper and learns more about the Chamorro, the indigenous people of Guam. To really know and experience Guam, one has to leave the glitz of Tumon and venture "down south" where you can still see and feel the traditional culture of the people of Guam.

Guam is much more than a United States military outpost and Japanese playground. It is home to one of the most adaptable and resilient people on the face of the earth. The Chamorro people have been colonized by three nations; first Spain, next the United States, then the Japanese, and finally the United States again. When we think of a colonized people, we most often think of the British in East and West Indies or the French in Algeria or Vietnam. We rarely conceive of *modern day colonization.* Yet, for over five hundred years, the Chamorro people of Guam have endured and still suffer the indignities of colonization.

Guam is the southernmost island of the Marianas, geographically and culturally part of Micronesia. The peace of this lush, fertile territory, home of the Chamorro people was first breeched with the arrival of Ferdinand Magellan, the Portuguese explorer, who captained a fleet of Spanish ships. Magellan landed on Guam in 1521, but Guam was not declared a Spanish territory until 1565, when King Philip II ordered explorer Miguel Lopez de Legaspi to take possession of the Philippines and all of the islands encountered during his voyage. It was at this time that Guam and the rest of the Mariana Islands were claimed by Spain.

In 1668, over 150 years after the arrival of Magellan, life would forever change for the Chamorro people when the first permanent Spanish settlement was established with the arrival of Catholic priest, Padre Diego Luis de San Vitores. These first missionaries initially sought to persuade the Chamorro people to accept the words and faith of *Jesus* the Christ, when this failed they resorted to violence and force. Battles raged throughout the Marianas as the Chamorro fought to preserve their way of life and their lands.

From 1680 to 1695, a war of extermination was waged against the Chamorro. With the deliberate introduction of diseases like smallpox and syphilis, the Chamorro population was almost decimated; their numbers were reduced from 80,000 in 1688 to below 5,000 in 1741. The survivors, mostly women and children were removed from their traditional lands and relocated to villages where missions were established.

The Chamorro women displayed remarkable adaptability and resilience as they were subjected to unconscionable brutality by the Spanish. The Spanish administrators had total control over the lives of the indigenous population. An administrator could even assert his right to "have his way with" a bride before her and her husband could consummate their marriage.

By 1783 only 1,500 of the ancestors of the present-day Chamorro remained. The Chamorro adapted the religion and the conditions lain down by the Spanish missionaries and administrators. They displayed a tremendous resilience of spirit however. Despite the oppression and brutality endured, the Chamorro people maintained their language, their herbal medicine, and most significantly their belief in the ancestral spirits.

When the United States declared war against Spain in 1898, the Chamorro would get a new colonizer and end Spain's the 350-year rule. A result of the Treaty of Paris of 1898, Guam, along with the Philippines, Puerto Rico, and Cuba were ceded to the United States. Of the four, only Cuba has been able to assert its sovereignty and independence.

Under the new United States colonization, Guam was administrated by the U.S. Navy and naval captains were assigned to serve as the governor of Guam. The Chamorro were colonized by the United States until 1941, when they were abandoned by the U.S. preceding an impending attack by the Japanese. When Japanese warplanes arrived to bomb U.S. military installations and ships on December 8, 1941, almost all U.S. military dependents had already been evacuated from Guam on October 17, 1941.

After the surrender of the U.S. forces in Guam, the Chamorro would endure colonization by another foreign power. They lived under Japanese occupation until 1944. Life for the Chamorro became incredibly brutal when U.S. warplanes began bombing Japanese installations in 1944. When it looked as if the war was turning the tide favoring the U.S., Japan moved a battle-hardened division from China, one that been fighting for ten years, to Guam in order to prevent Guam from being used as a staging area and launch site for attacks on the Japan mainland. Upon their arrival, the Japanese occupation turned very brutal. During this period, the Chamorro were forced to march to concentration camps and mass executions and other atrocities occurred.

In August 1944, the Chamorro were "liberated" from Japan by the United States. This liberation would prove to be "bittersweet". For the fourth time, the Chamorro people would find themselves colonized and relocated from their lands to village centers prescribed by the colonizers. Under the U.S. liberation, Chamorro lands were appropriated to build military facilities and bases. To this day, Chamorro who were the owners of this land are denied access to their property and have never been fairly compensated. Guam went from being totally self-sufficient, growing a large variety crops, grazing cattle, and having a strong fishery through the Japanese times, to now where 85-90% all food is imported. Because of the loss of land and the lack opportunities to make a living in the new economy, more the Chamorro live in the U.S. mainland than on their island.

With each successive colonization the Chamorro people would have to adapt to the rules set forth for them by those foreign to their ways. They have been required to learn Spanish, Japanese, and English over the last 500 years. Alien religious, social, and political systems have been thrust upon them. Yet the Chamorro people remember the wisdom of their ancestors and seek to regain a sense of their true identity.

Two days before the *traveler* departed Guam, she spent the evening dining, drinking wine, chewing betel nut, and conversing with a group of Chamorro "militants". A "militant" is what you are known as when you attempt to overthrow the bonds of oppression and colonization. As the *traveler* listened to the plight but also the courage and persistence of these people in their quest for sovereignty, she realized that she would never view Guam in the same way. Beneath the surface, away from the military installations and the tourist attractions, there resides an indescribable force; a people empowered by the spirits of their ancestors who yearn and will continue to struggle for freedom in the face of insurmountable odds. While the Chamorro people have learned to adapt to the rules and the ways of three sets of colonizers, the thirst for the freedom that theirs by birthright will never be quenched.

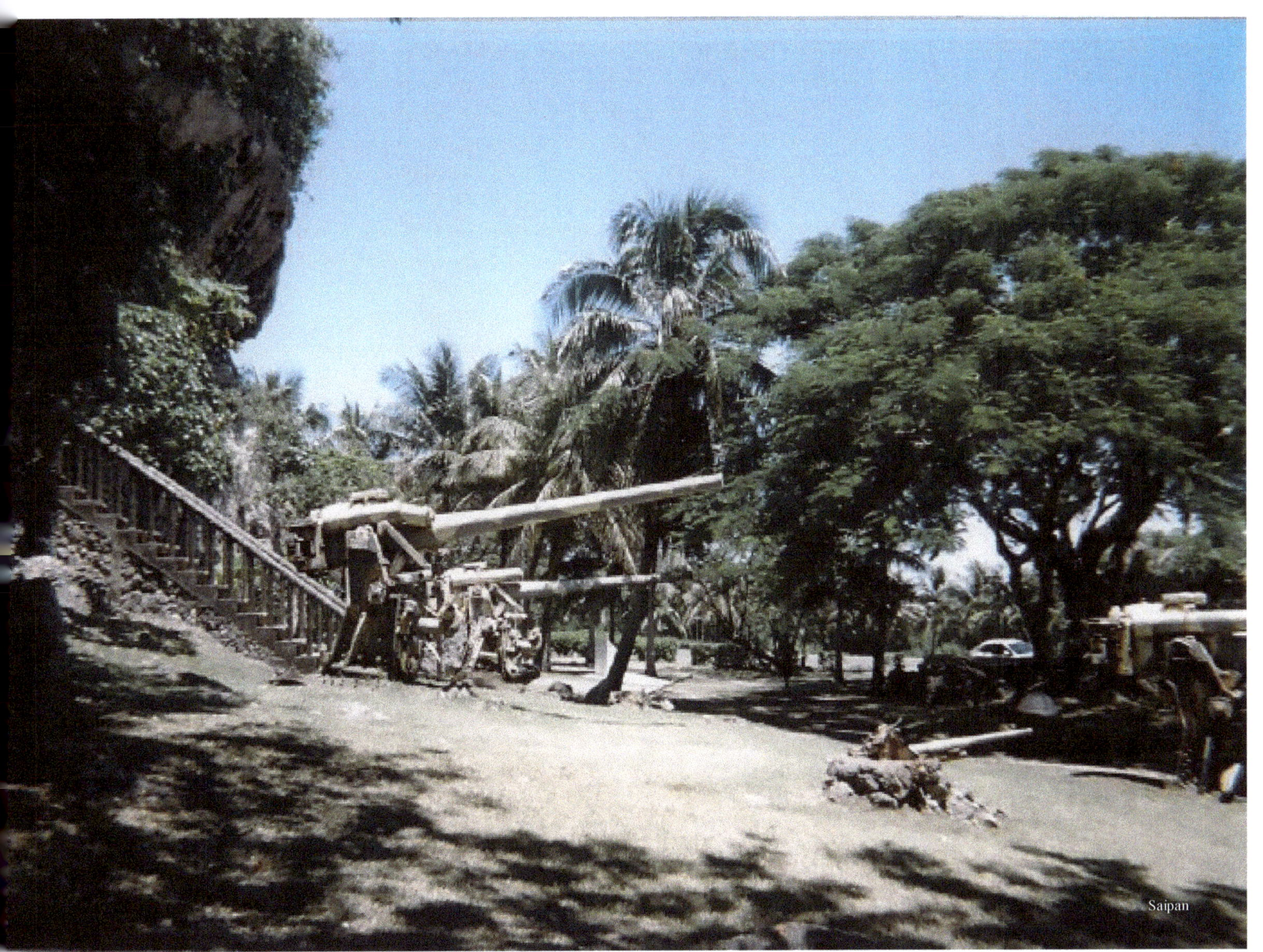

Saipan

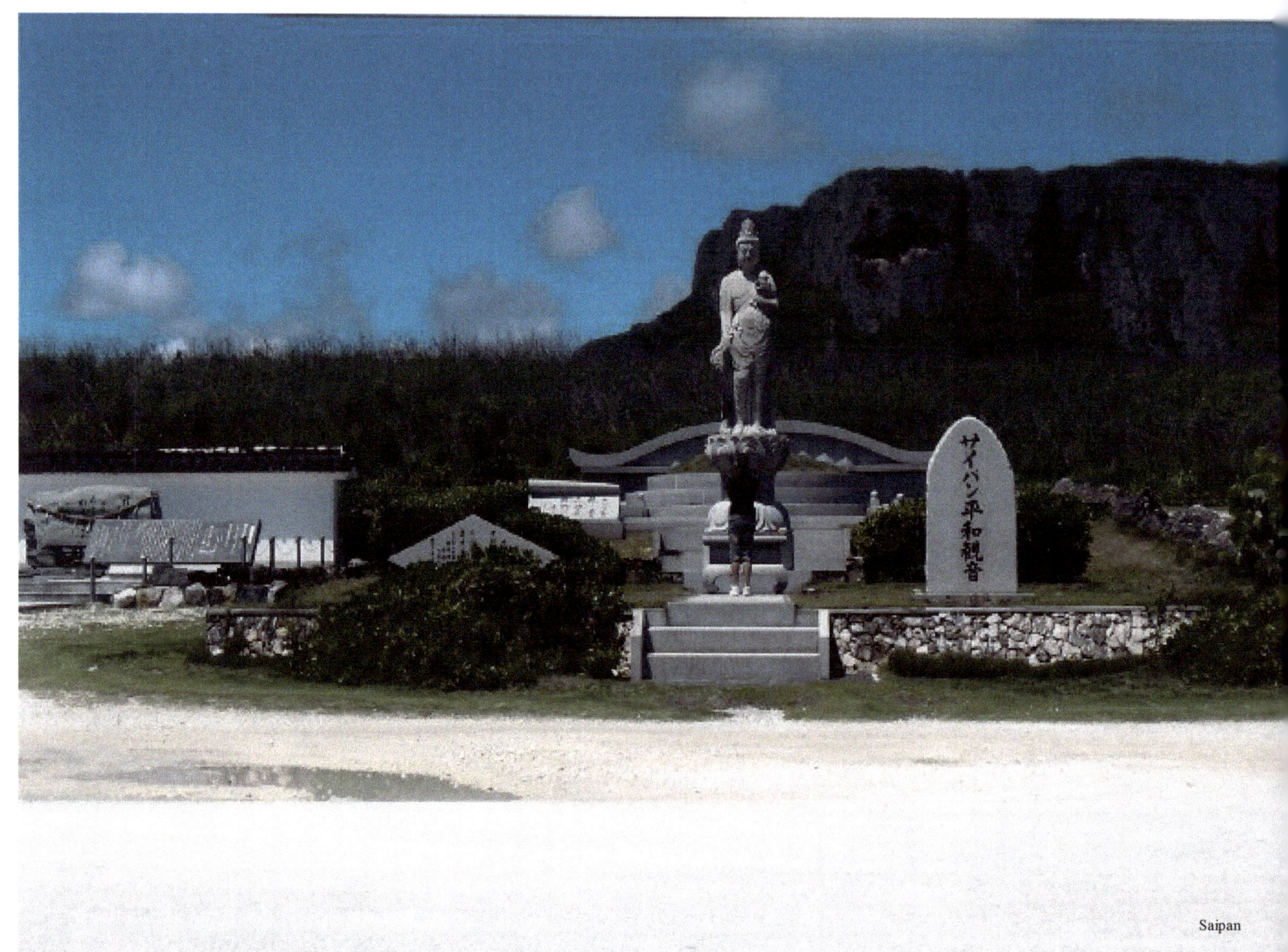

Saipan

A PLEA FOR PEACE

After a 30-minute flight from Guam, the traveler arrived at Saipan International Airport. The traveler was giddy with excitement and expectation. Just the name "Saipan" conjures up images of an exotic island, warmed by Pacific breezes, flowered with lust vegetation, and bordered by tropical beaches .Finally, I am here, on this island paradise, the destination for Japanese, Chinese, and Korean tourists. Saipan unfortunately, also, has the reputation for having sweatshops and large red-light district. By the time the traveler arrived, however, the garment industry was essentially extinct on Saipan.

Saipan is an island of enormous beauty. It is surrounded by a stunningly deep blue ocean, decorated with the magnificent "Flame trees", and crowned with beautiful mountain vistas. The sunsets on Saipan are breathtaking. It is hard to imagine that such a beautiful serene island could be defaced by the brutal acts of war. It is not the beauty of the place for which Saipan is known, it is for the fierce battles to control this island that took place some fifty years ago during World War II.

The gentle island peoples who first inhabited these islands have only known domination since the first Europeans arrived on their shores in the 16th century. First they endured the brutality of the Spanish, then the island (these human beings) were "sold "to Germany by the Spanish after their defeat in the Spanish American War of 1898. With Germany's defeat in WWI, the League of Nations by mandate "awarded" this island, to Japan in 1919. Saipan was occupied by the Japanese until 1944.

It was the Battle of Saipan, that burned the island into history books. From June 15, 1944, until July 9, 1944, the battle for control of Saipan waged. It is ironic that the battle was not fought by the native peoples who had inhabited the islands for thousand of years but between two nations who either occupied or desired to occupy the island for the purpose of "strategic advantage". This battle would prove to be disastrous; a very high price was paid both in terms of military and civilian deaths.

At the end of the battle, almost the entire garrison of Japanese troops, estimated to be 30,000, and 22,000 Japanese civilians perished.

Far from the glitzy upscale shopping district with its Hard Rock Café , Hyatt, and luxurious resorts that one discovers the meaning of the events that occurred on Saipan. Two sites on the island in particular are monuments to the total insanity of war. At Suicide Cliff, some 800 feet tall, hundreds of Japanese soldiers jumped to their death rather than surrender. Banzai Cliff, is even more heart-wrenching. On an absolutely beautiful bluff overlooking a deep blue ocean, men, women, and children plunged to their deaths. It is said that the entire civilian population of Saipan committed mass suicide by jumping off cliffs or with hand grenades in caves.

Words cannot describe what the *traveler* felt as she stood on the very spot where these human beings, whole families, perished. She can only imagine the hopeless stares of parents and the confused cries of children during those last moments . As each family made the ultimate sacrifice, hundreds more who had joined the somber march, the "funeral procession" from town to the Cliffs and waited their turn.

As one stands here, peering out into the endless sea that swallowed this mass of humanity, you realize that you are not alone. At least 8,000 souls call out from their watery graves and beseech us to stop the madness; to learn from their sacrifice that war is truly insanity; that there is no victory in war. Both the victors and the vanquished are wounded permanently and if not by physical death, die as devastating a spiritual death.

Monuments to peace line the road leading to Banzai Cliffs. They ask all who visit to retreat from the insanity of war and to claim peace for mankind. One monument is to the Goddess of Healing. As the traveler laid an offering and poured libation she asked for the healing of the consciousness of those who would flame the fires of war; for the healing of the consciousness of separateness, of individualism, of the sense of superiority, the need for empire; for the healing of excessive desire, materialism, and consumerism, all of which lead to the need to dominate, to exploit, to oppress others; and finally for the healing of the consciousness of us, the majority, who like sheep do not raise our voices in protest and who offer our young as sacrifice.

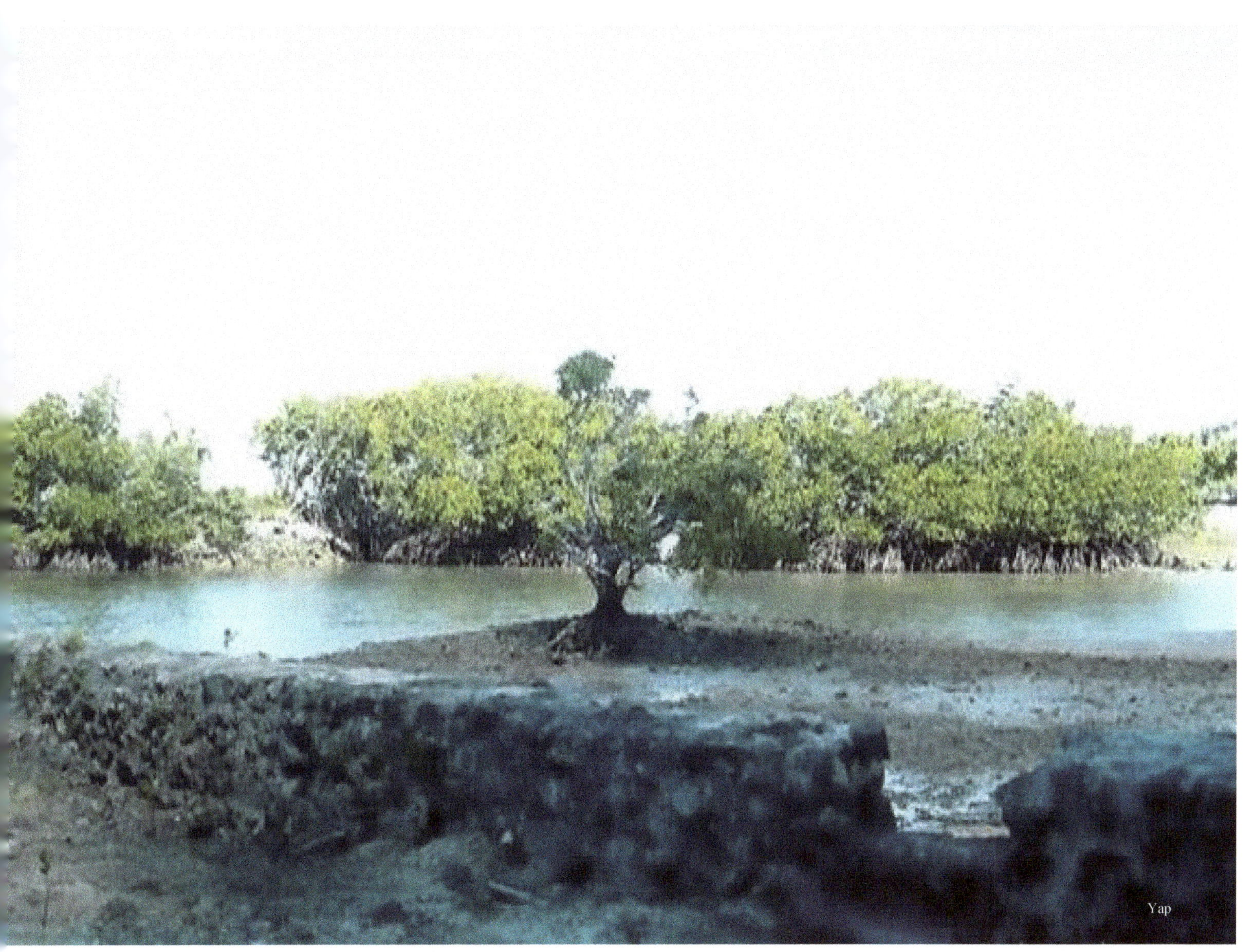
Yap

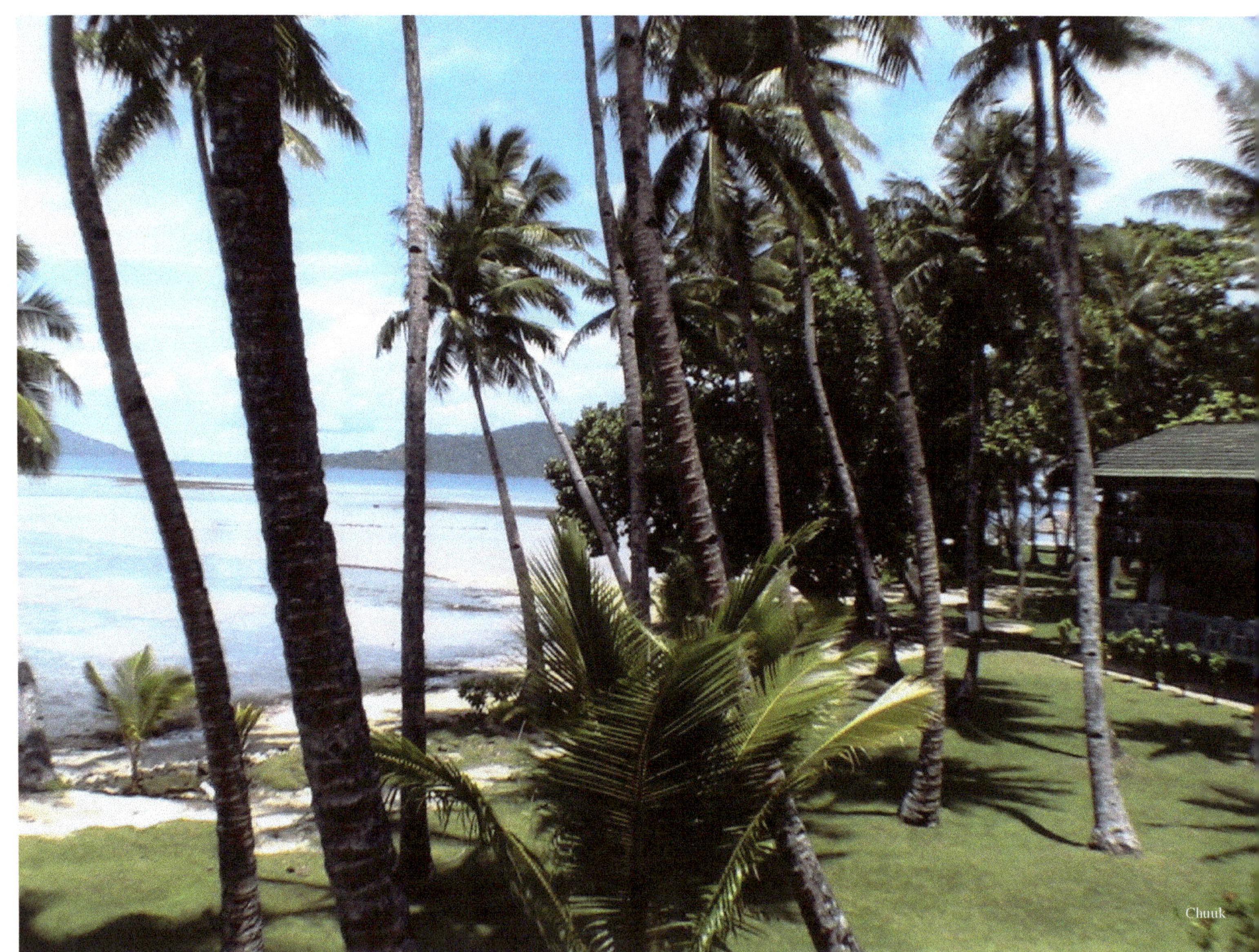
Chuuk

DÉJÀ VU

Riding down the main road that flows through Moen, on the island of Chuuk, the traveler had the distinct feeling of having experienced this place before. The manner and the movement of the Chuukese was reminiscent of many of those, especially the men who inhabit "colored towns" in the rural south of the United States. From the swagger of the men to the ubiquitous gold teeth, the Chuukese and rural southern blacks have some mystic connection.

The traveler would discover that the Chuukese and blacks in the United States had even more in common than mannerisms. Like blacks in the U.S., Chuukese are the victims of a plethora of myths and stereotypes with historical roots. Chuukese men were stereotyped as being angry, violent men as early as the 1800's. Today, the entire island is stigmatized.

Chuuk has the distinction of being called "the sinkhole of Micronesia". It is considered to be a backward and ill-managed place. According to Western standards, everything about the island is substandard. The poorest in capital income of all the surrounding nation-states, Chuuk is characterized as being debt-ridden, incapable of collecting taxes and fees, run by incompetent administrators who mismanage funds. The public school system is considered to be substandard and the health care system inadequate.

Visitors to the island are warned not to go out at night or to patronize the local bars because of the potential for violence. Historically, Chuuk has been known for its violence; in earlier days, violence occurred between different clans. Today, because of the dollar economy and changes in the clan and family structure, more intra-family violence is seen. Not unlike poor blacks in the South in the United States, small clubs or bars, known as "juke-joints" in the U.S., are places where men gather on payday, drink, gamble, and release pent-up frustrations that often lead to fights. This behavior is to be expected of men who have lost their identities, and who are attempting to adapt to new economic, political, and social systems.

The stereotypes of Chuukese follow them as they migrate to other islands. When Chuukese migrate to Guam, they fare poorly. They tend to be the most impoverished group, to do poorly in school and to be overly represented in the criminal justice system. Chuukese males on Guam like black males on the U.S. mainland have the reputation for being violent and engaging in criminal activity. On Guam, the Chuukese represent the perfect profile of a low caste group; the expectations and their treatment results in a self-fulfilling prophecy.

So what is the cause of the "Chuuk problem" as it is called. It may very well be that the Chuukese are caught in a severe "crisis in values". A crisis in values occurs when the traditional cultural and social norms of a group are in the process of being destroyed and the group has not adapted to the new, foreign cultural norms. The Chuukese in many ways appear to be resisting all attempts to "remake their culture".

The traditional lineage system, independent villages, and family responsibility probably account for what appears to be "ineptitude" and "corruption" by government officials. The movement from a land-based to a dollar economy with the disruption of family life and confused identities brings with it a vast array of social problems. To expect anything less is to see this situation in very naive and linear terms.

Despite the problems caused by the crisis in values that they are experiencing, the Chuukese in many respects, are "their own people". Even on Guam, they are easily identified as they wear their traditional clothing, speak their own language, and adorn themselves with tattoos and gold teeth. Perhaps it is this holding on to who they are, their unwillingness to totally remake their culture that presents a problem for the Chuukese. It may very well be that the "Chuukese problem" is their refusal to conform.

The Chuukese may be the freest people in Micronesia. The stereotyping of them in the 1800s was done of course by those who wanted to colonize then and control their islands. Their lack of desire to participate in being colonized gained them their reputation of being (literally) "out of control". In their history, leadership never was higher than village chief. When an artificially constructed government was placed on top of them, they cannot be who they are not; they have a very long lineage as a village leadership-based people. Because outsiders desire them to conform to the system that they do not consider relevant to the lives – living with this system has not improved their life condition because of the vacuum that has now formed in between a broken system of traditional leadership and a foreign system of governance that is administered poorly. This occurrence in very common in the "developing world". One is which before subjugation by a foreign power, a culture is a well-functioning and sustainable society based on system of familial and clan obligations. In order to establish the relevance of a new system of government and to break any power structure that may affect its rule, traditional leadership must be subverted. For the foreign power, this may serve the purpose of weakening local leadership but it does not address the reality of continued familial and clan obligations. Because these new systems of government are imposed and based on foreign value systems and worldviews that are often at odds with the worldview of the subjugated people, there is a very steep learning curve in terms of developing proficiently in at running these new systems of governance. Because these new systems are run ineffectively base of the lack of institutional knowledge and/or cultural incongruence in the core guiding philosophies of these systems of governance, the new systems end up being used to meet the traditional system of familial and clan obligations that the old system is now no longer able to meet.

Just because an outsider desires to remake people into its image, it does not necessarily mean that these people will do so. Subjugating their long-proven working social organization for a foreign one, which, as one can see in the present day financial and environmental crisis' in international news daily, does not being relief for the masses, only pockets inside of its walls. The Chuukese see no reason to be experimented on. Chuuk's "wildness" makes it an unattractive destination for outsiders with nefarious intentions. They will ride this present group of outsiders just like they did the Germans. Except for the stories that people tell in the oral tradition about the "German Times" and a few humorous dances mimicking the marching style of German soldiers, there is virtually nothing apparent left in their culture or society that would ever lead one to believe that the German's ever colonized Chuuk. In the same way, "country" black folks from the rural south, act "crazy" for the same reason. During the most violent days of Jim Crow governance in the rural American South, and even somewhat afterward, there were only two ways that a black person could be free – in death and in being deemed "crazy".

“Crazy Negroes” were generally left alone by the white authorities, while those not deemed crazy lived under a regime of terror and oppression. This reality was quite well known by black folks in the rural South. Once deemed crazy, your family would have generally have a free pass to live as you wished by yourself, because “crazy negroes” did not believe in the system, therefore could not be coerced through fear. Physical violence would have to used to subdue these people, and whenever conflict escalates to physical violence it become a risk to both sides. To establish “craziness” one would have to have an altercation with the authorities. You would either be killed or you would live freely, deemed “crazy”. The Chuukese may just be the “Crazy Negroes” of the Micronesia.

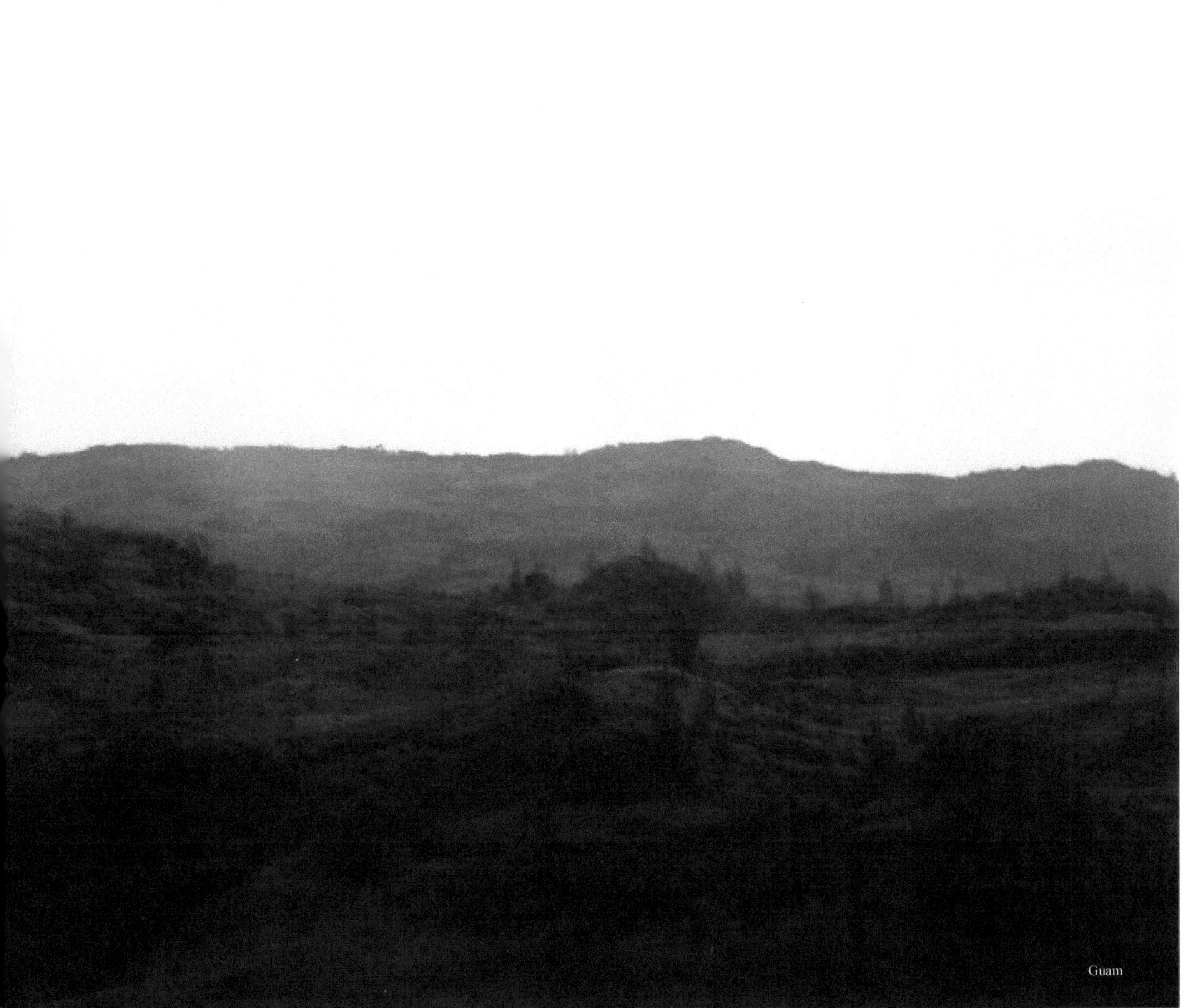
Guam

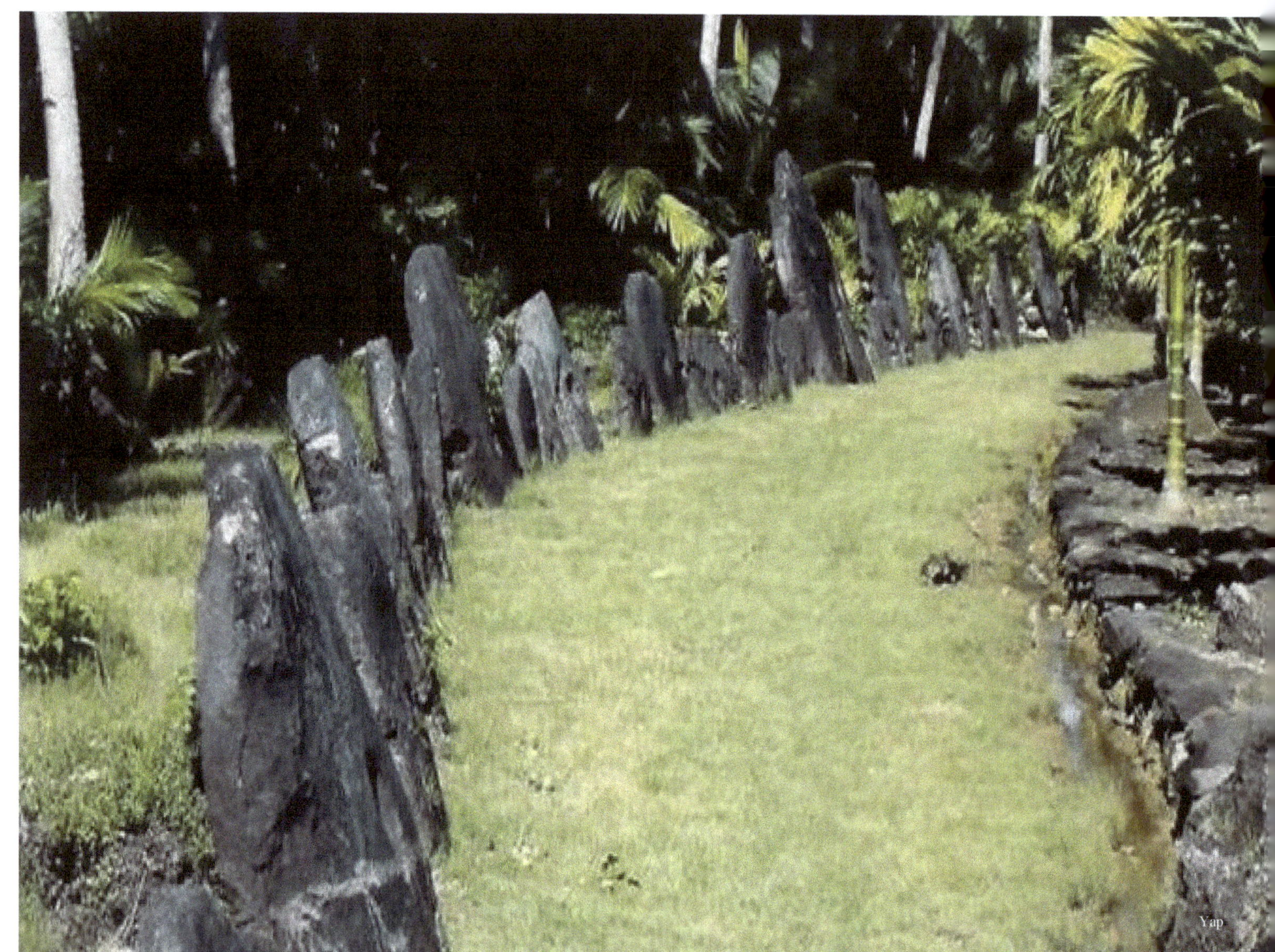

Yap

HOLDING ON TO THEIR TRUTH

In June, 1668, with the arrival of six Jesuit priests, the spiritual lives of the Chamorro people would be in a significant way forever changed. Before the arrival of the missionaries backed by the military might of Spanish soldiers, Chamorro had a rich spiritual life that included the spirits of nature and most importantly, those of their ancestors. Chamorro practiced ancestor worship and placed the skulls of deceased ancestors on altars in their homes.

The Spanish missionaries regarded the religion and culture of the Chamorro as pagan, heathen, and superstitious. Believing in their own superiority and the rightness of their religious dogma, for thirty years, through the process of "reduccion", the Chamorro were forced to adopt Spanish customs and to become "devout" Christians. The peaceful message of Jesus the Christ was brought to the gentle people through brutal and violent means.

The initial efforts to convert the Chamorro are said to be relatively successful although resistance followed persisted for almost thirty years. The process of cultural destruction began almost immediately with the conversion process. In the initial stages of "Christianizing" the values of individualism, separation, exclusion, and false superiority were introduced to a people whose culture was experienced as collectivism and oneness   The new Christians were treated differently; they were given privileges not allowed the others such as being the first allowed aboard the Spanish ships to trade.

 The new religion further eroded core aspects cultural life of the Chamorro. The bachelor houses, the traditional dress or lack thereof, sexual mores, and dances were considered licentious. The skulls of ancestors were crushed and spears made of the leg bones of the deceased were burned.

The greatest impact of the new religion, however, was on women. Traditionally, the Chamorro society was organized matrilineally. Inheritance was passed down through female lines; women were in charge of the household and made all of the major decisions. Christianity, however, preached male dominance, with males in control of home, family, and property. With Christianity, women were to submit in all things and lost both their social and political power.

Catholic churches adorn almost every corner in Guam but the conversion of the Chamorro people to Christianity was not a matter of free choice. The Chamorro were forced to submit to the loving, peaceful message of the Christ. For the Chamorro, the presence of the "men of God" meant domination, brutality, and violence. While the Chamorro were forced to attend church and preached the Gospel of Jesus, they were subjected to beatings, burned villages, destroyed crops, and even death. The Chamorro people learned the lessons of Christ through power and guns.

At the reduccion process, the Chamorro lived as good Spanish subjects and devout Christians. From all outwardly appearances, the culture of the Chamorro that conflicted with Christianity had been destroyed. What the traveler discovered on her last visit to Guam however, was that Chamorro beliefs in the spirits of nature and of their ancestors had survived Christianity.

As she dined with friends, there was much talk of "Taotaomona"; the spirits of the ancient Chamorro people. These spirits reside in the mountains and jungles on the island. The traveler was warned to always be respectful of the Taotaomona and to as permission before entering any area in which they dwell. Those who disregard this advice pay a price; they can discover marks and lumps on their bodies, become ill or even die. These are not the beliefs of the superstitious, the poor and uneducated, but of most Chamorro who understand the true nature of spirituality.

By the time of the last battle between the Spanish and the Chamorro, the population had been decimated and they had been forced to accept Christianity. The spirits of their ancestors did not desert the Chamorro however; some four centuries later, the spirits of the ancestors survive, provide protection, and demand reverence.

To be able to know and understand the spiritual nature of all things is to be truly blessed. Spiritual knowledge requires the believer to surrender to something higher and greater than that perceived by the five senses. Indigenous peoples and those able to live spiritually in the fullest sense are often ridiculed by Western thinkers as primitive and superstitious. However, those who are connected to Spirit are able to maintain that connection despite the dogma, admonitions, and even the persecution of organized religion.

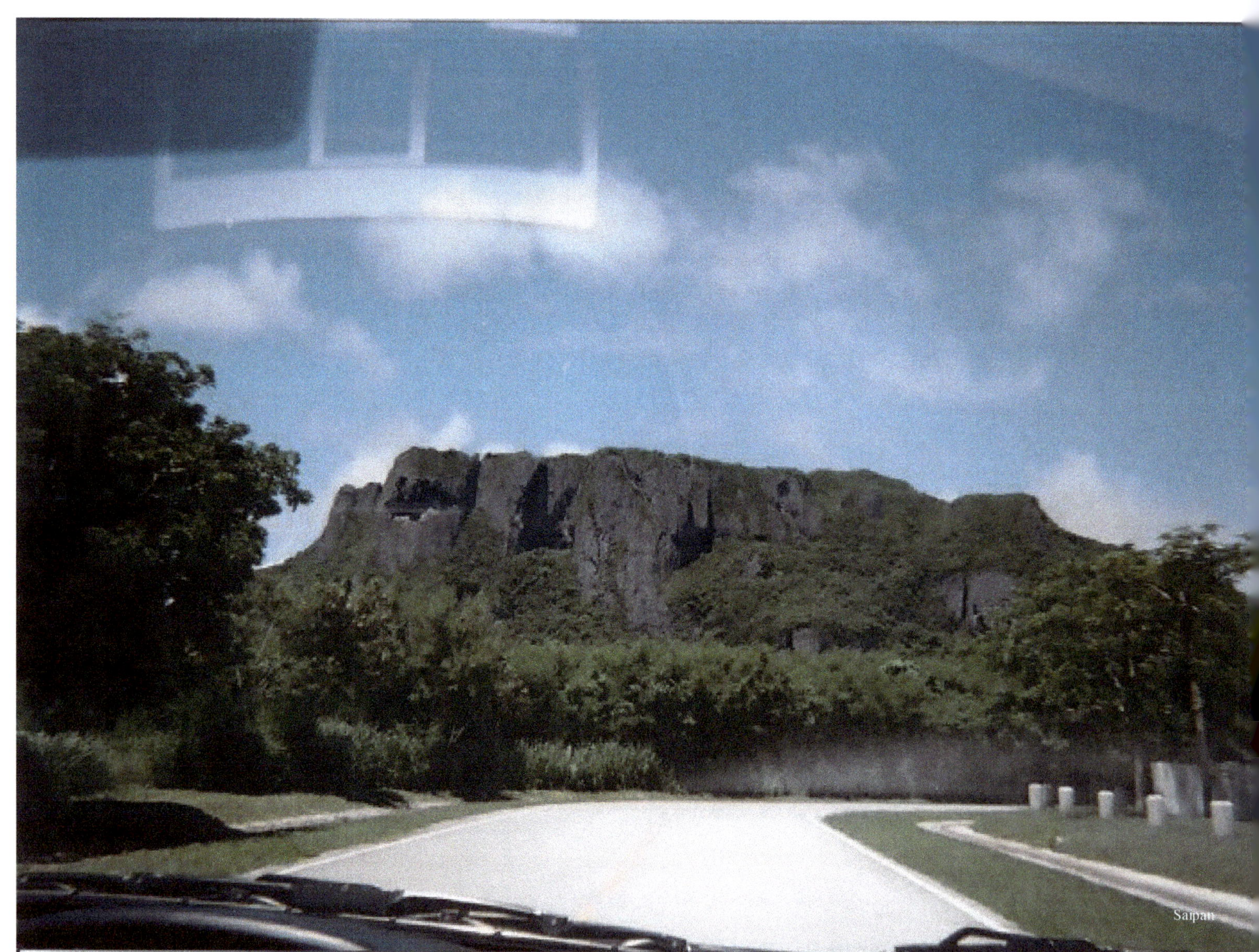
Saipan

A SHAMEFUL PAST

The traveler had only one thing in mind as she took the seven-minute flight from Saipan to her sister island of Tinian. Like most of the Japanese, Chinese, and Korean tourists who come here, the traveler wanted to try her hand at "lady luck". Tinian these days is best known for the opulent and expansive Dynasty Hotel and Casino. One enters an enormous but elegant lobby and immediately views the huge glittering chandelier that hangs above. The 75,000 square feet of casino floor is loaded with all types of games; the traveler however, a risk taker in most other things but not in gambling, retreated to the slot machines. The experience proved not to be economically enhancing in the least bit.

Tinian, like Saipan, is a beautiful island, with rugged shorelines and lust vegetation. Basking in the luxury of the Dynasty Resort and taking in the beauty of the island, one would hardly believe the events that gave this island its somber distinction. This beautiful, tranquil island is famous for being the base which atomic bombs were dropped on Japan. On August 6, 1945, "Little Boy" was dropped on Hiroshima, and three days later on August 9, 1945, "Fat Man" exploded over Nagasaki. The events that took place on this island changed the world, changed the notion of how we fight wars, and forever changed our sense of humanity.

On the island of Tinian can be found the ruins of the House of Taga. Chief Taga was one of the chiefs of the Mariana Islands during the pre-Spanish occupation. The native peoples were considered by the Spanish and all who came after them to be primitive, in need of Christianizing, and civilizing. One can only wonder, however, what Chief Taga would think of modern man and his conception of civilization. Is the dropping of an atomic bomb on other humans more civilized that killing your enemy with spears and poison darts? Is it more cowardly to strike your enemy from the air that to face him in hand to hand combat? Is there a moral code by which war is to be fought? Wars are as old as man himself, but it seems as though men like Chief Taga would never have had the desire or the will to consider war as a means by which all humanity could be destroyed.

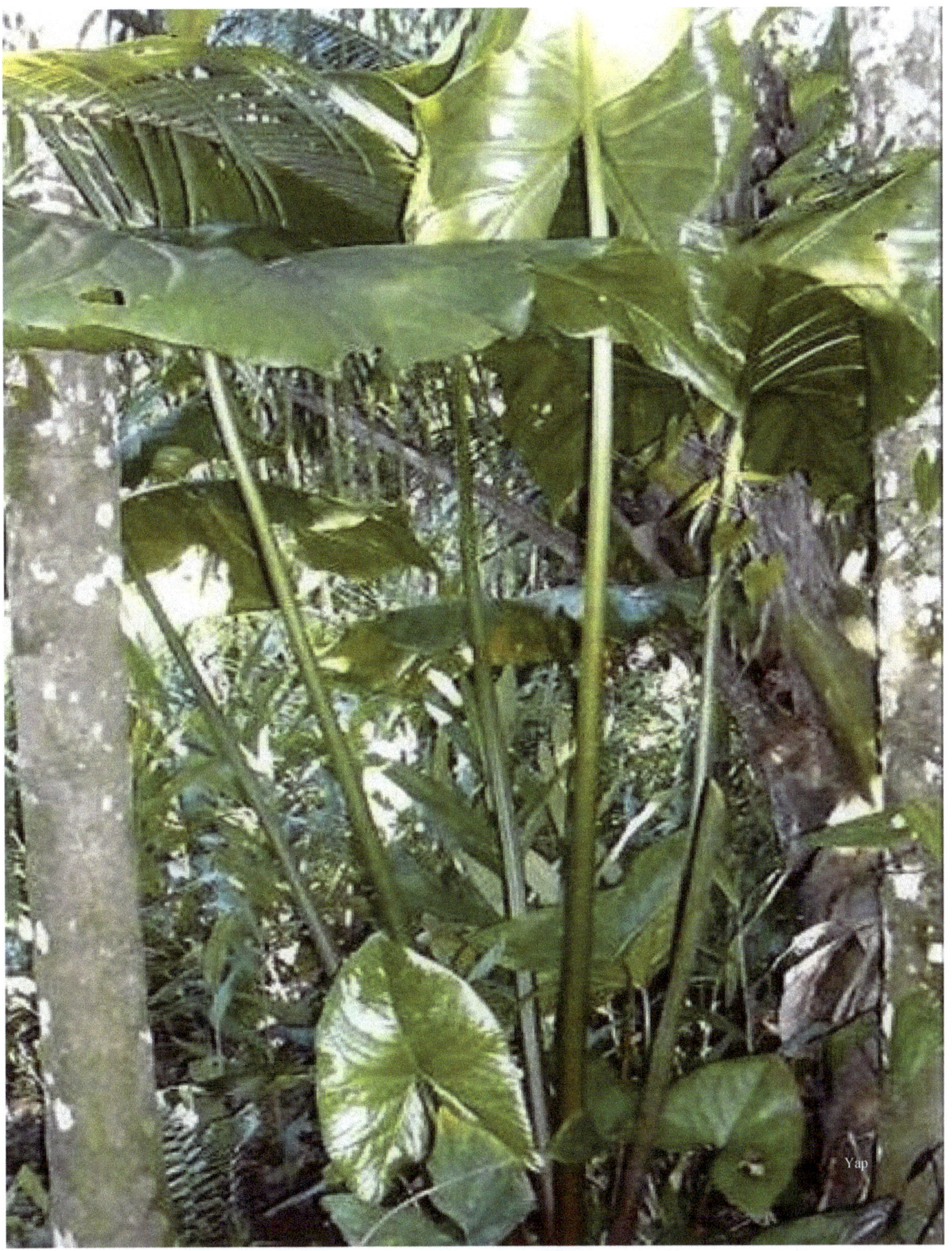
Yap

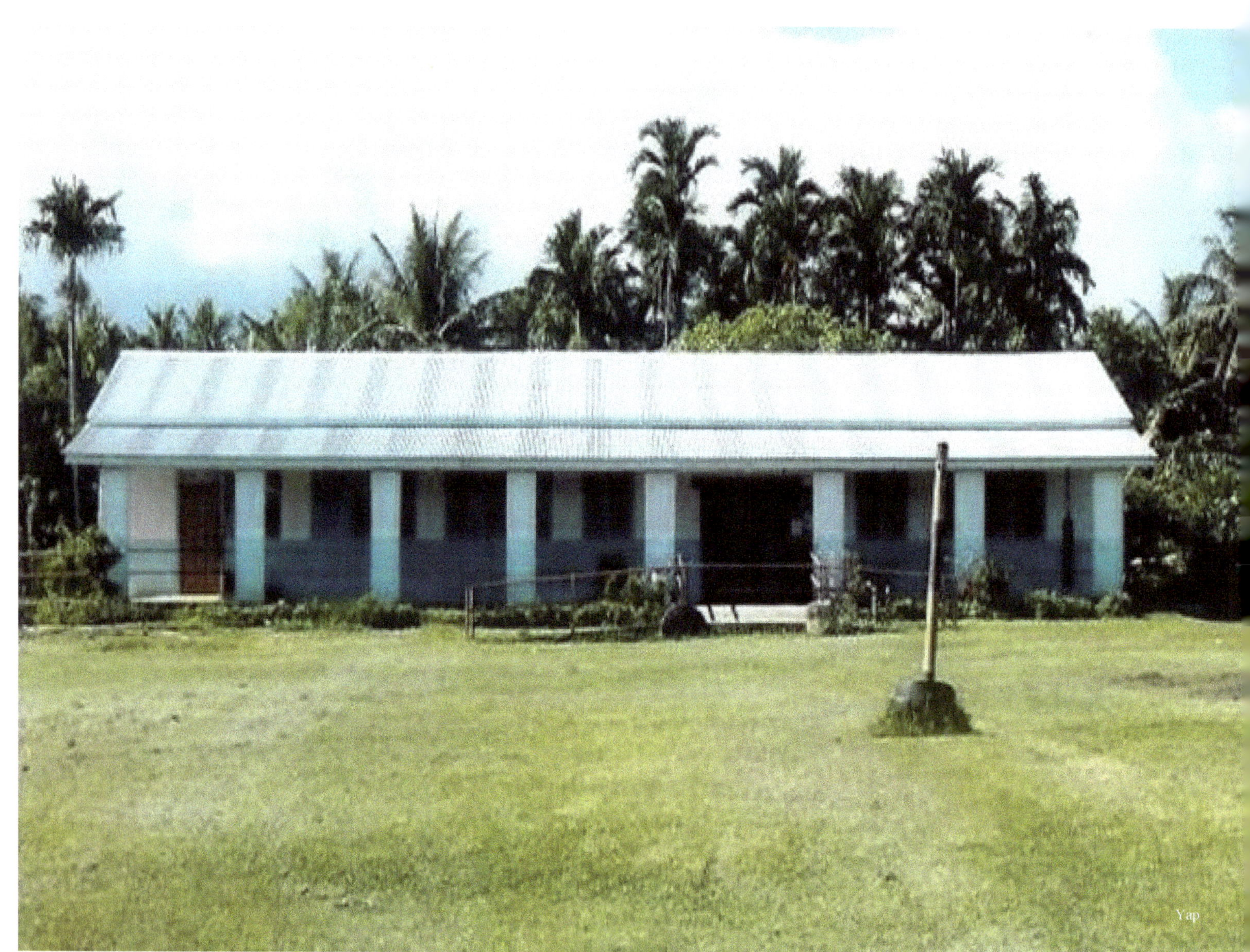

Yap

WOMEN POWER

If there was anywhere to have come of age as a woman in recent ages, it was in Micronesia. They did not need liberation, they were liberated. They held social and political power (behind the scenes) and were sexually free as well. Much of the power that women traditionally held in Micronesia were eroded however with the coming of Christianity and Western paternalism.

The power that women held came from three basic sources: the matrilineal order of the society; the complementary roles of men and women; and the protection afforded women by the extended family.

Margaret, a Palauan woman, is one of the most powerful women that you can encounter. Her sense of person power comes from growing up in a matrilineal society. The adopted daughter of a chief, Margaret is the embodiment of a powerful woman. Margaret's sister, a school principal who thoroughly enjoys her betel nut is an equally self-assured woman. When the traveler visited Margaret, she and her sisters were in the midst of making important decisions about which piece of land that they would give to their brother. As protectors of the land, Margaret and her sisters were empowered to decide who would or would not be given land in their kin group.

The very distinct but complementary roles of men and women in Micronesian society give equal status to the work done by both men and women. Men and women had separate but equally important roles to play. The work of both women and men was integral to the survival and welfare of the family and community. Unlike Western societies where women's traditional roles of childrearing and caring for the house are often denigrated, the role of the woman as child bearer, as the child's first teacher and the transmitter of the culture was crucial.

Political power is shared with men and exercised by women in traditional Micronesian society in subtle but significant ways. While men are involved in "public life", ratifying and discussing important decisions, it is women who initiate the planning of what will be discussed by men. Women in traditional Micronesian society also held the distinction of having the role of peacemaker. Women could actually force men to make peace by meeting with other women, arranging the terms of peace, and informing men of the details of the peace arrangement. When women can stop men from engaging in war, that is power!

Changes impacting Micronesian society such as the dollar economy and the disintegration of the extended family have had a devastating effect on women. Domestic abuse is rampant. Women who used to have the protection of their brothers and uncles in the extended family now face the wrath of often drunken husbands alone. As couples marry and move away, the women are left isolated and defenseless.

The dollar economy has forced many women into the workplace. They no longer have the time or energy to assume the role of first teacher and transmitter of culture. Some like Delores, a teacher on Yap, laments not having the time to adequately take care of her taro patch. She fears the lost of status because her patch is neglected but must manage both her job and traditional responsibilities.

 Teenage pregnancy is a concern to many on the islands now. Girls no longer have the benefit of "women's secrets" as taught by women in traditional society. They are copying images of women from foreign sources such as Western television; they are learning "how to be women" but of course not powerful women . There is a lot that can be learned from traditional Micronesian societies about how women can experience and be empowered without having to burn bras and demonstrate. Women like Margaret understand what the good life for a woman is all about.

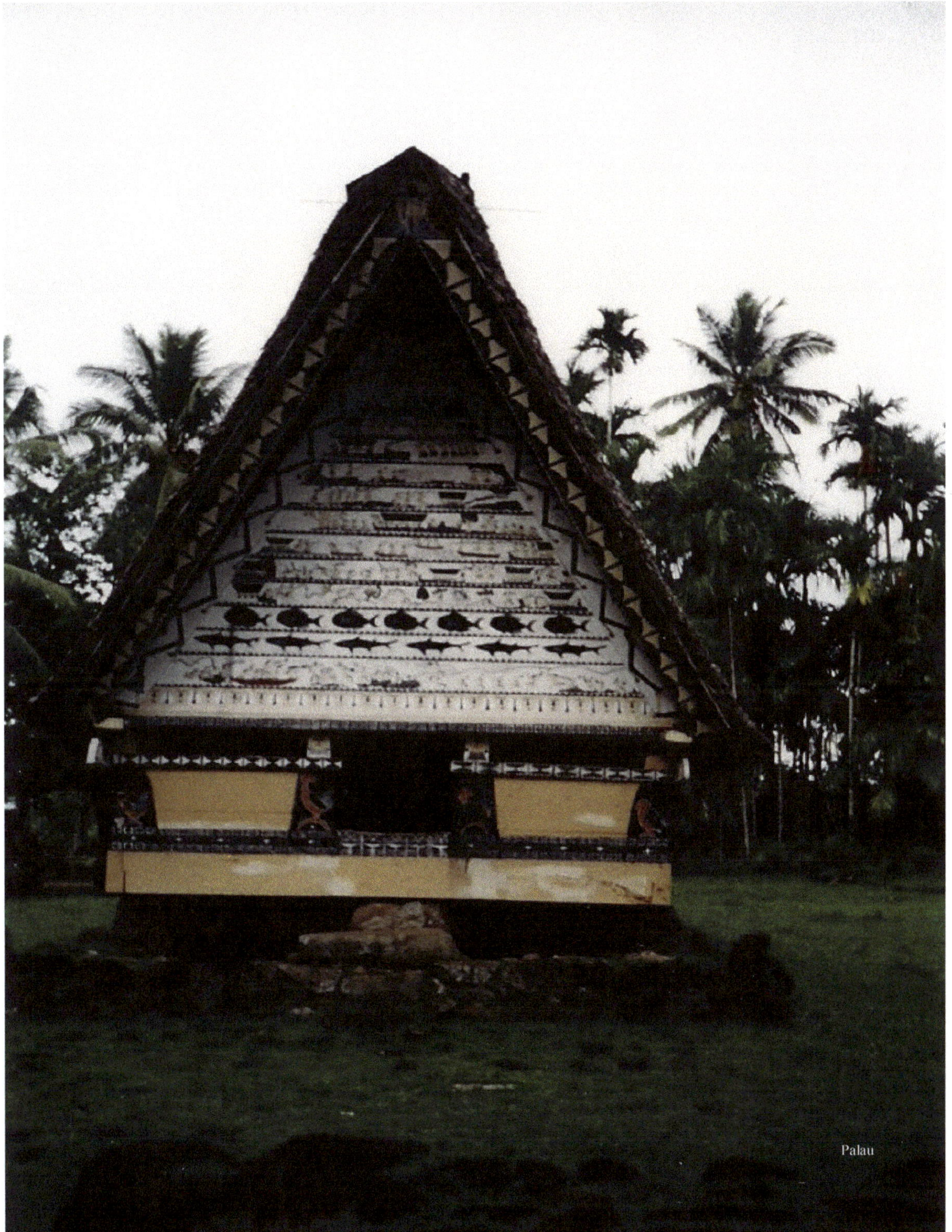

Palau

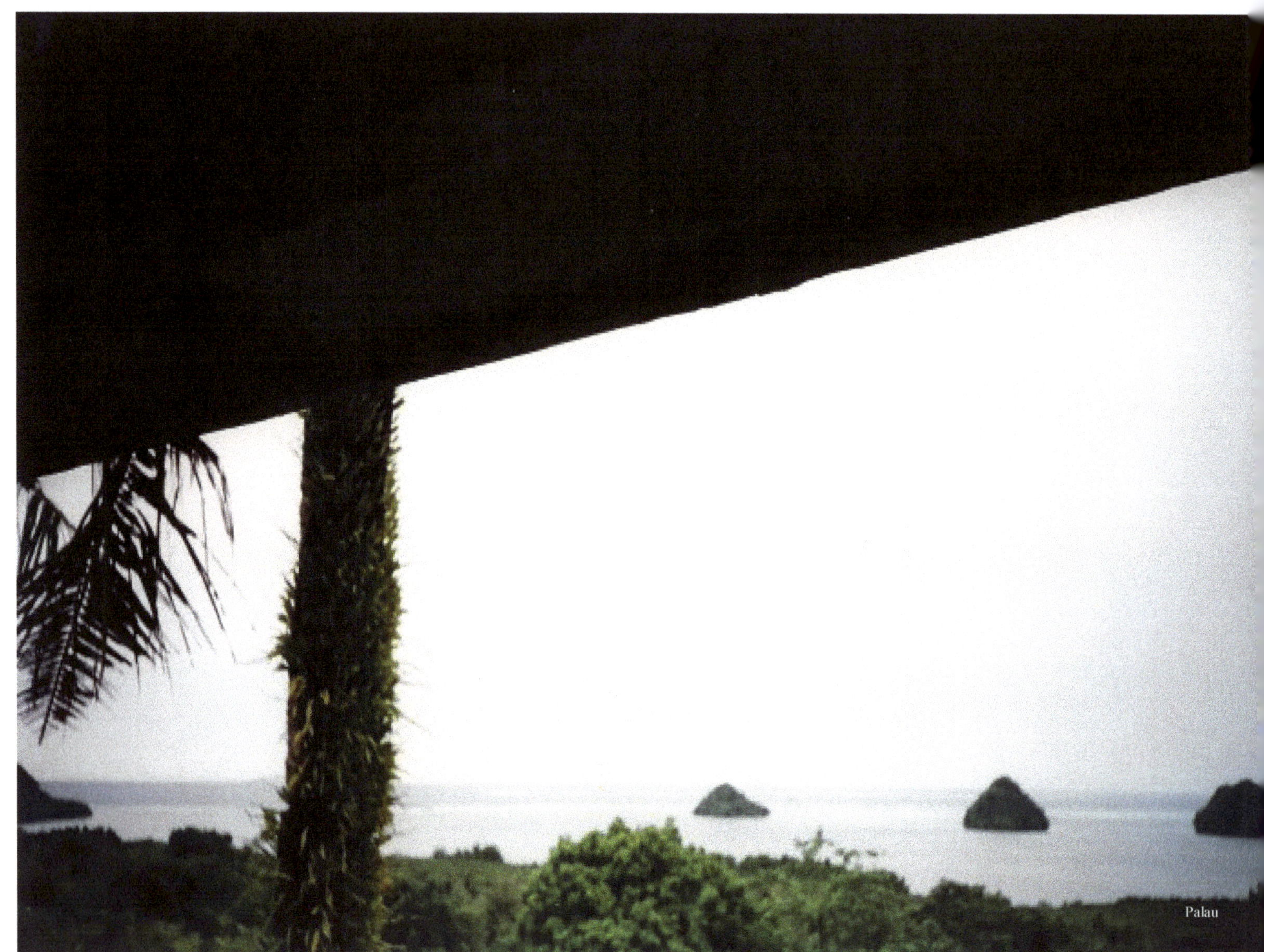

Palau

KEEPERS OF THE FLAME

Palau is one of the world's youngest and smallest sovereign nations. Previously, it was one of four United Nations Trust Territory districts administered by the United States. It gained its independence in 1994, with entry into a Compact of Free Association with the United States. Palau has a 95.2 % literacy rate and is one of the wealthier of the Pacific Island states. Perhaps, a key to the promising outlook for Palau is the independent spirit of its people. In a sense the people, have spirits as solid as the Rock Islands for which it island is famous.

The people demonstrated this independent spirit when they voted against joining the Federated States of Micronesia. They cited language and cultural differences as reasons to remain independent. In 1994, they voted to "freely associate" while maintaining independence from the United States. Even more remarkable, in 1981, the Palau people voted for the world's first nuclear free constitution. For this act of autonomy and sovereignty, the U.S. would not agree to a Compact of Free Association. The island was not granted independence until the anti-nuclear clause was repealed.

Despite the challenges faced by being associated with a colonial power, one aspect of the independent spirit of the Palau people remains. The Modekngei religion, a syncretism of and traditional Palauan religion and Christianity persists. The religion was founded in 1914 after the Japanese occupation. Its key aspects are healing and prophetic oracles.

The religion which now boasts a school built in 1974 has survived in spite of prohibition, the harassment of followers, and the imprisonment of its leaders. Modekngei which had its largest following during the war years has been considered to an anti-Japanese religion by some. The Japanese attempted to discourage the practice of the native medicine, prohibited the religion, and jailed its followers and leaders repeatedly. The new occupiers from the United States were equally opposed to the religion. The main complaint of the U.S. was that the medical practice of the religion interfered with the native use of the U.S. Naval medical facilities.

This religion outlawed by the Japanese and opposed by the U.S. was "anti-" neither Japan or the United States. It was strictly a force by which a segment of the Palauan population sought to resist the cultural destruction that was occurring to its people. The major tenets of the religion reconnected the Palauan people with their cultural center or essence. Its goal was to make the Palauan people who shared a common core of ancient values into a cohesive unit. They emphasized the pre-foreign values and customs of the Palauan.

There is a fallacy promoted by all would be masters that the population of the targeted group is childlike, pliant, passive, helpless, and dependent. The culture is characterized as primitive and undeveloped . This paternalistic view justifies the domination of the group and the attempts to "remake the indigenous group into the colonizer's image". Any attempt by the indigenous group to maintain their cultural center is always opposed by the colonizer.

Religious syncretism is always an act of rebellion, an act of defiance of the oppressive order. Holding on to any aspect of what is a group's own in the face of oppression is an act of cultural assertion that poses a threat to the new order. Whether it is Santeria in Cuba or Modekngei in Palau, the religion serves the purpose of maintaining some sense of cultural self. When outlawed by the authorities, this cell of cultural assertion moves underground and still operates to meet both the spiritual and political needs of the group.

The Palauan people's desire to operate as an autonomous nation and to seek a new way of existing as an anti-nuclear nation may have been dampened by the more powerful United States. In any group of people, however, there will always be a segment of the population, like the Modekngei, who guided by ancient values,   will keep the sacred trust of the ancestors.

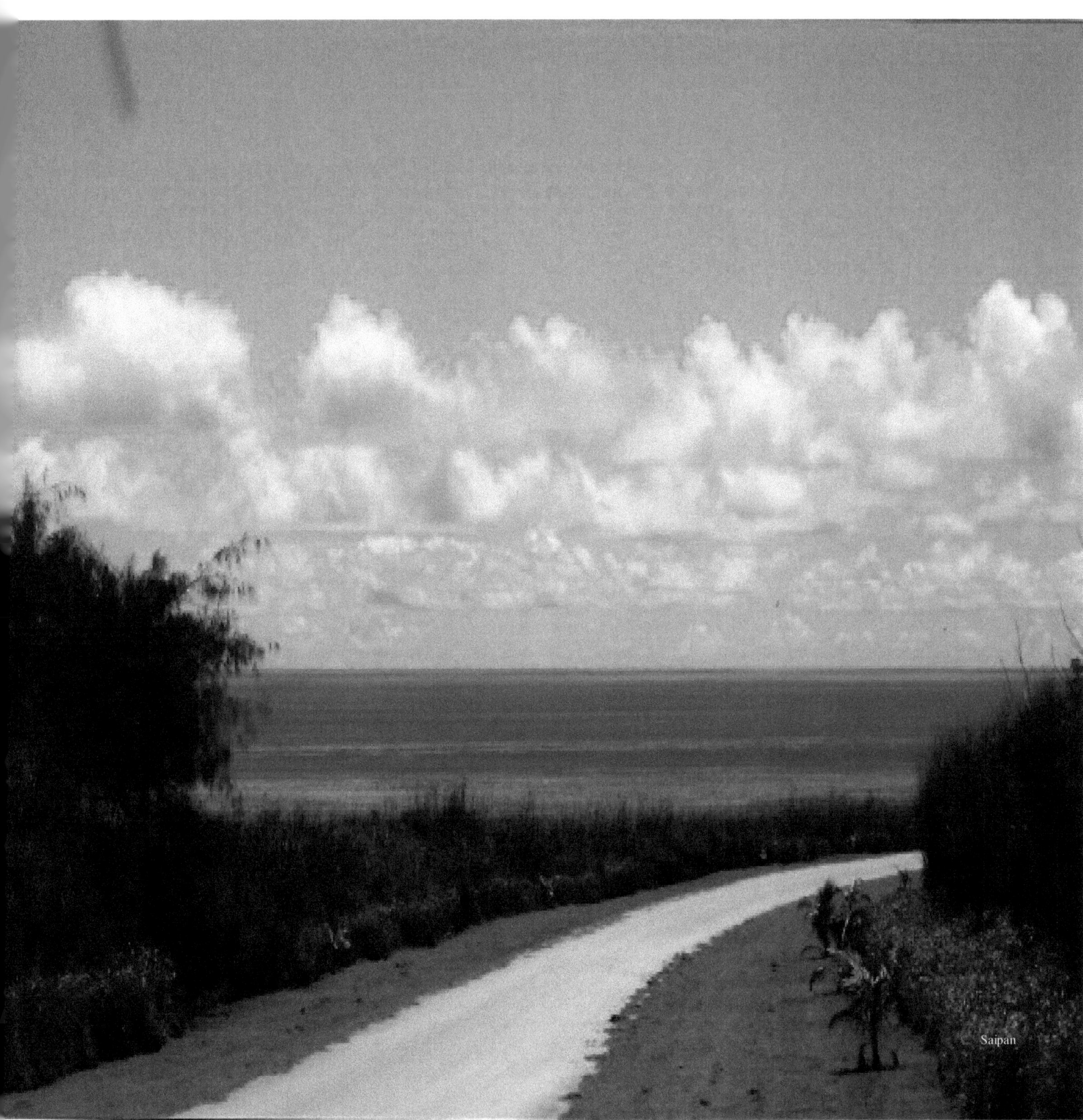

Saipan

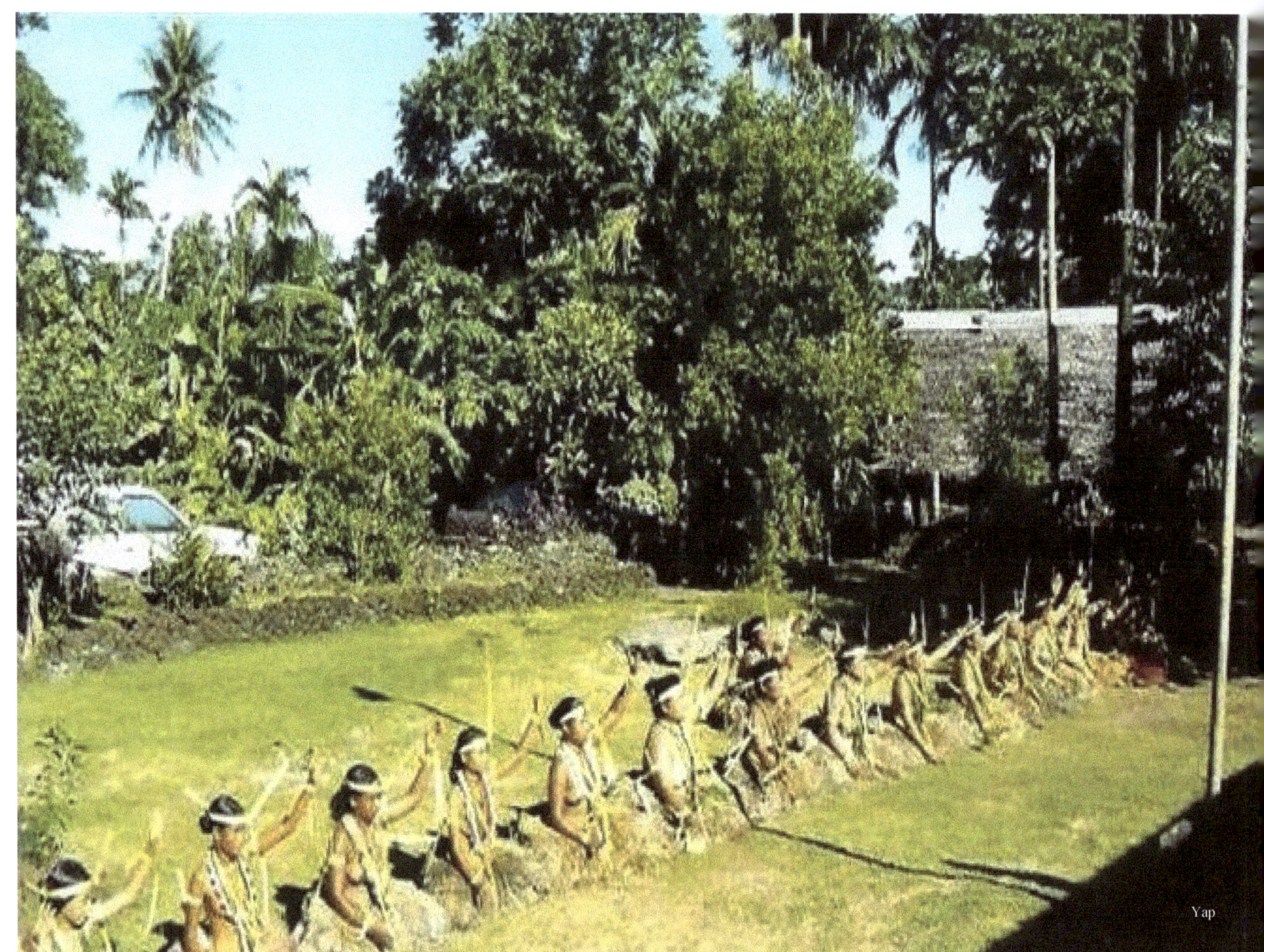
Yap

MAINTAINING THE WAY

There is no more beautiful or impressive sight than sunrise on Yap. The entire sky is bathed in deep orange and gold highlighted by streaks of blue. It is truly magnificent. Waking up to this sunrise alone lets you know that you have stumbled upon a treasure. Much more awaits on Yap however, as who takes an journey into the good life.

The Yapese notion of a good life is one of harmony - harmony with nature and harmony within one's family, kin groups, and community. The society and its rules are structured to ensure that harmony is maintained. Westerners often erroneously believe that a traditional life such as the one lived on Yap denies individuals of their creativity, esteem, and personal identity. Esteem and identity are derived from one's group affiliation and the arts and customs are testament to the creativity and ingenuity that exists and thrives in this environment.

Individualism protects the rights of some and encourages individual pursuit of goals no matter what the consequences to others. The way of the Yapese is to protect the rights of the individual within the context of the group. The Yapese have devised a system of rules based upon the virtue of respect ensure harmony between villages. The Westerner might not understand these mandates and even regard them as silly or inconsequential, but they do what cultural norms and mores do, they serve the needs of the cultural group.

One such rule requires that one walk single-file, in the center of a rocky path, while never looking into the villages that one may pass on the way. First of all, the path is designed so that one must pay attention as they walk; they must look down to watch one's step. The stones that line the center of the path are of irregular size and shape. Not looking into another's village as one passes is a sign of respect, but equally important, this mandate is meant to reduce human jealousy and to prevent one from coveting what does not belong to him or her. A wisdom that comes from a ancient understanding of human nature.

Another custom is to be sure to carry one's basket or to place a leaf under one's arm when approaching and passing near another's village. These are signs that one comes in peace. Always, the ultimate sign of respect is to ask permission to enter another 's village. There might be much less conflict in the world if simple rules of conduct such as these practiced on Yap were known and practiced by others in the world. Perhaps it is a standard of group behavior such as this that truly ensures individual well-being.

Collective responsibility is the Yapese way. Selfishness is highly frowned upon within Yapese culture. It is expected that everyone will be involved in the weekend cleaning and repair of community houses (both for males and females). Individuals who do not participate are considered to be selfish and ostracized. First, the may be warned about their behavior, if it does not improve, the individual will be fined; The ultimate punishment for selfish behavior is to be asked to leave the village.

Yap is structured along strict caste lines. The work that one does in the village, and whom one may marry are dictated by caste lines. But, in these modern times, allowances are made. The traveler encountered a couple from different caste groups who were eventually allowed to marry. The husband was from a high caste group and the wife a lower caste. The couple fell in love and wanted to marry but no matter how much the husband pleaded with his father and cried, the father said no. Finally in an act of desperation, the husband ran away to the wife's village to live. The father eventually relented and the couple was allowed to marry. This act of marrying out of his caste could have had dire consequences for the young man as disobedience could have cost him his name, land, and place in the family. This is one crack in an otherwise traditional way of life.

Yap is the most traditional of the islands in Micronesia. Many of the traditional customs remain but there are indications of cracks in the good life on Yap. Addiction to Western foods laden with sugar, salt, and fat are taking a toll as lifestyle diseases such as diabetes, heart and kidney disease are on the rise. The village system of guiding and disciplining children has broken down as on other islands in Micronesia. Now among young men coming home from school, one can see "western wannabe's", sporting the hairstyles, clothing, and mannerisms of popular music stars seen on television.

One individual, John Mangefel, now deceased chief and former governor of Yap, understood the ways in which the Yapese were slowly losing their good. He refused to wear ties and other western clothing, wore flip-flops to state meetings, carried and chewed his betel nut everywhere he went. John decried the influence of the school and the western values that it taught. He spoke passionately about girls going to school and coming home pregnant. Like other aspects of traditional culture that have been lost, the menstrual houses and women's secrets that young women were taught are no longer part of the Yap's cultural practices. John was a very respected leader; hopefully his urging and pleas to maintain the Yapese way will ensure that like the sunrise, the good life on Yap will be eternal.

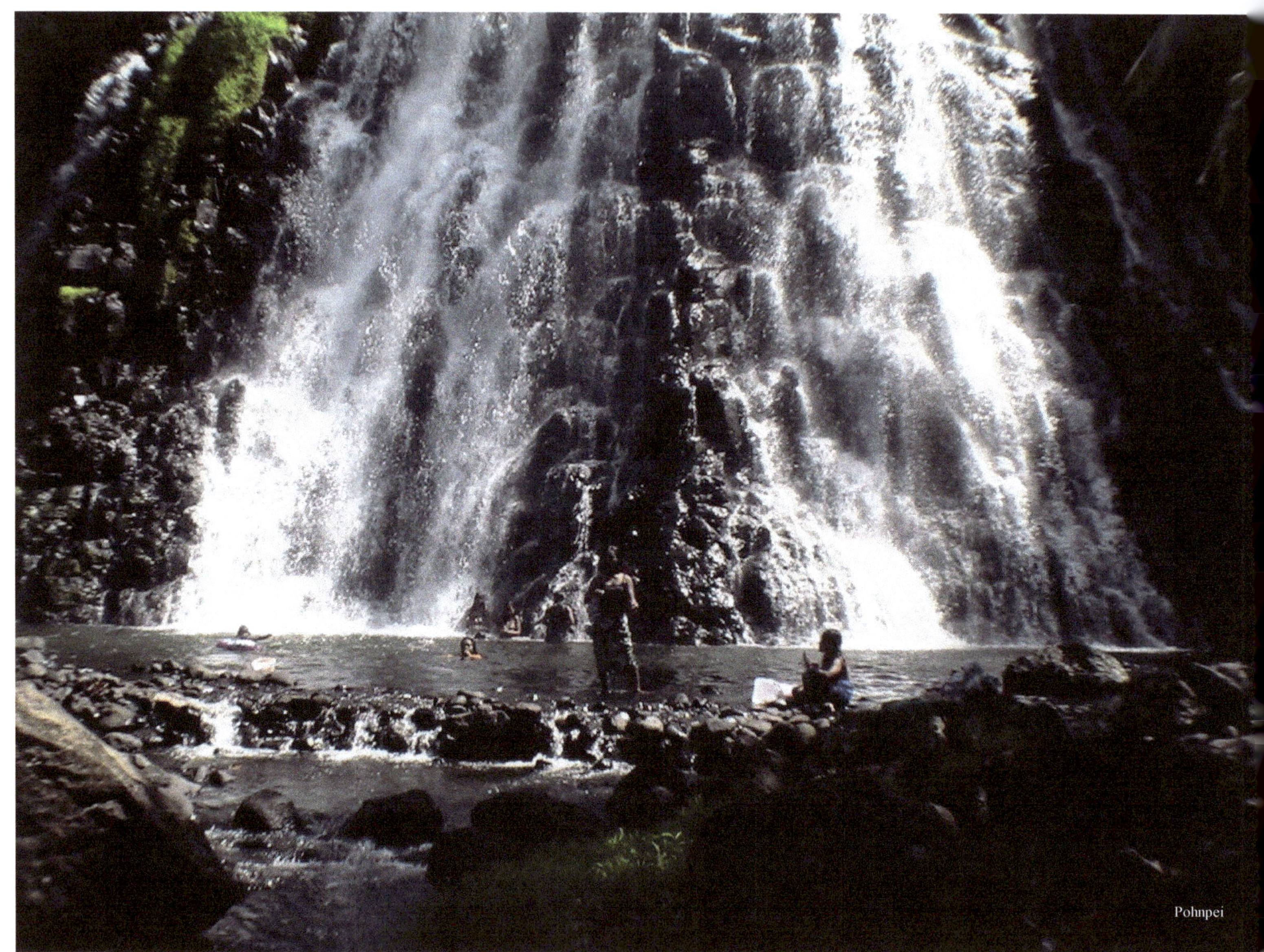

Pohnpei

THE HEALING WATERS

On a visit to Pohnpei, after a trip to Nan Midol in the morning, I wanted to spend the afternoon at one of the seven famous waterfalls. In my way down to the pool at the bottom of the waterfall, I slipped on the rock on which I was climbing and fell, cutting my foot in the process. It was not bleeding profusely, but enough to be a little concerned. So, I decided that it would be ridiculous to go back without spending some time in the waterfall. Little did I know, that cutting my foot was my entré into understanding the magic of the waterfalls. When I got in the water and starting swimming around, I jumped up frightened because a fish was biting the skin where I cut my foot. I began to swim again, and again a fish came to nibble at my foot. My thoughts at this time were that the fish saw that dangling flesh as a meal and that they were intent on eating my foot. After awhile I decided that I would get out, because this foot-eating thing was a bit too much.

Not to long after, on Guam, I went to get a massage, and the owner of the spa told that they had a masseuse from Pohnpei, and asked if I would be interested in having her do the massage rather than the Chinese acupressure massage that I had received before. I agreed. It ended up that she was a fourth generation traditional masseuse. All of the women in her family were masseuses. Like in Guam, traditional massage could cure a large variety of ailments that one would not think massage could of in the same way that people accustomed to western medicine are surprised by the results of chiropractic adjustments.

Well, while I was receiving my massage, I mentioned that I had gone to Pohnpei and was sharing with her my experiences there. At some point I got to the story about the fish that was trying to eat my foot at the waterfall. She asked where the waterfall was, I told her describing the direction we took after getting back from a morning trip to Nan Midol. She laughed, and said, "the fish was not eating your foot; it was healing you."

She then asked me if I saw the person at the side of the pool feeding the fish and eels. I thought about it and realized that I did see someone at the side of the pool sitting the water, but it had no relevance to me at that moment, because I was worried about fish biting my foot. She laughed again and said that there is an agreement between the people and fish at the waterfall – that humans will not eat them and in exchange, humans will feed them and they will heal humans of their skin ailments and other diseases that they help cure via the skin. She said that everyday a designated person sits down in the water and feeds the fish and eels. The eels even crawl all over the person. Eels normally will bite someone, but not in the waterfalls because there is a relationship between humans and the animals in the water. In present day, rather than fishing then bringing them some of the catch, the one who feeds the fish opens up cans of mackerel in the water and the fish and eels come to eat it.

She then told of a story of young woman who was the one designated to feed the fish at the waterfall near her home who died not too long ago. She was local princess and was designated as the one who was responsible for feeding the fish. She fed them for about a year, and then died unexpectedly. During the mourning period, the eels from the waterfall crawled from the waterfall to her house to pay homage.

Unlike what is often professed in the environmental movement, human beings are an essential part of nature, not innately a danger to nature. The question is more, whether groups of humans contribute to the sustainability of the areas where they live, or whether they are predatory and exploit where they live. Either role is acceptable in nature: there are sedentary groups and nomadic groups of plants and animals. The problems come when a decidedly predatory group does not keep moving, and plants its roots in a particular area, over time exhausting the resources of the area. Those who settle, under the laws of nature, have to contribute to the cultivation of sustainability of the area where they are living. For example North West Indian Nations live in the mountains and eat of the salmon in the rivers. When female salmon swim upstream to spawn and have difficult making it, the humans put the eggs in baskets and take then upstream for them to enable the cycle of life to continue. Another example is when human beings take care of bee colonies. By supporting the bees they support cross-pollenization of the plants in the area allowing for a rich diversity of genetic material in the local plant environment, the best possible method of fighting the impact of disease and pests on the plants in the community.

The relationship between the Pohnpeian people and the life in the waterfalls is an example of this symbiotic relationship between humans and the other life in the ecosystems where they reside. In truth, where they are humans who respect *The Way*, life is even more prolific and dynamic than it would be if humans were not there.

Ironically, I feel blessed to have cut my foot that day at the waterfall. Otherwise I may never have realized that fact that I was at The Healing Waters.

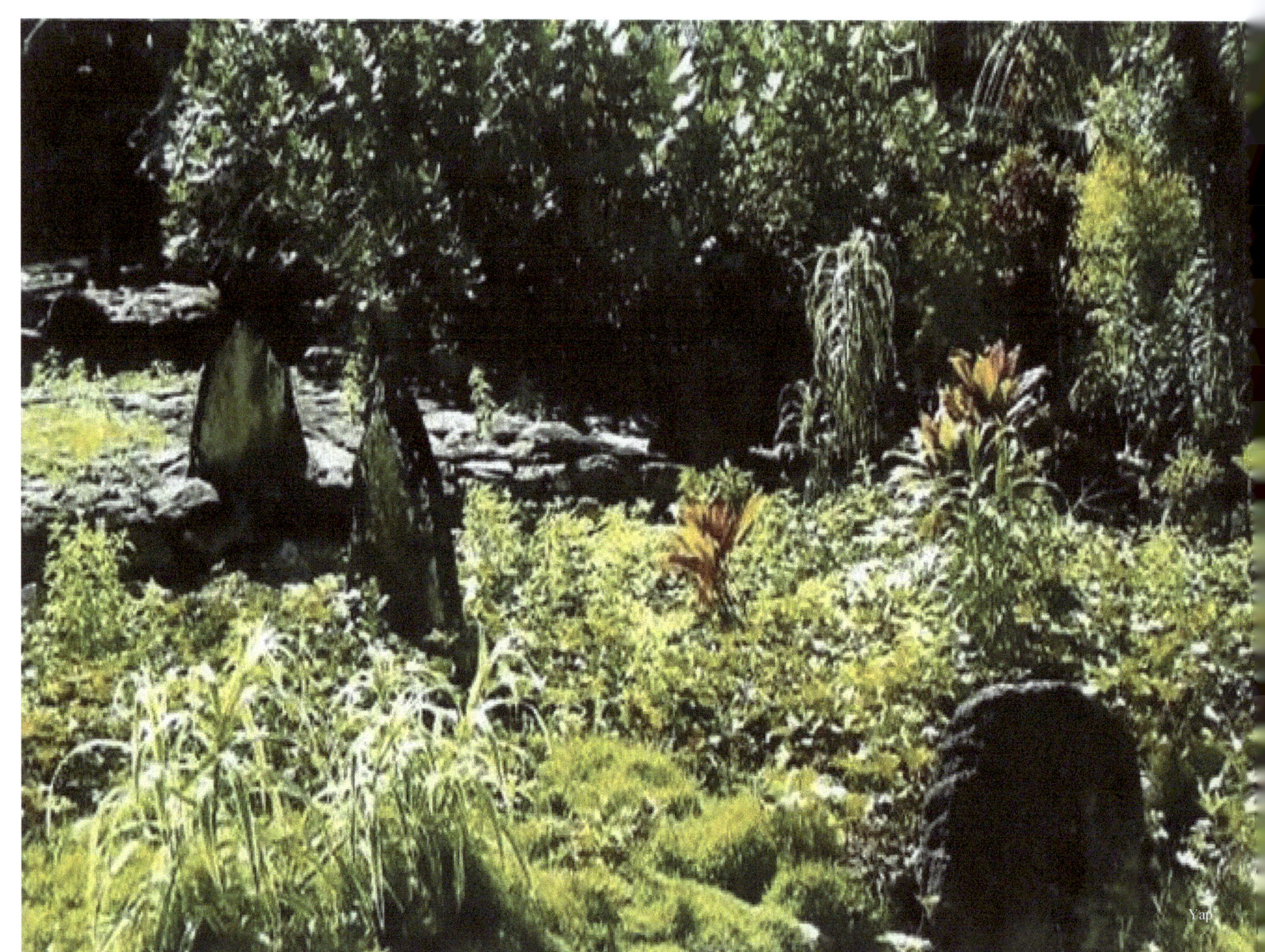
Yap

STAYING ALIVE

With the exception of Yap, all Micronesian societies are matrilineal. With the advent of Christianity brought by missionaries to the island first in the 1800s and again after WWII, the transmission of women's knowledge from elder women to younger women and girls was interrupted. As opposed to being whole beings grounded in the unbroken lineage of women's knowledge in the women's houses and for men in the men's houses situated on the women's property, continuity and sustainability has been maintained; but the interpretation of Christian marriage brought to Micronesia debases the "wholeness" of women and makes them into half persons whom could only achieve full personhood through Christian marriage; this marriage had to be headed by the husband despite the fact that he himself did not represent a family line, but rather his female relations. One could imagine what social chaos on a foundational level, not only to the matrilineal aspects of the society, but to the society as a whole.

Of course in matriarchal societies, generally women own the resources, and men decide how allocated resources are utilized, but with lessening matriarchal power and the constant reinforcement in the media of a patriarchal structure that is based on limitless consumption, rather than production and sustainability like in sustainable patriarchal societies like Yap, a woman rather than "being connected to a whole" becomes "valued as".

In contemplating the combination of outside forces that work against the integrity of traditional Micronesian cultures, I wonder if the reason why Yap to this day is the most traditional culture in Micronesia is because they are patrilineal and therefore women once married (in Yap proper) live with the husband's family and maintain continuity of women's knowledge like men's knowledge is maintained in matriarchal societies in Micronesia. As part of the social continuity, like land is controlled by women and passed to their designees throughout Micronesia (except Guam where the American authorities passed laws requiring women to take their husband's names and to later allow land to be sold to non-indigenous people).

The missionary ideal of modesty requiring women to have their bodies covered in long dresses is now endemic to Micronesian women, though exposed body parts traditionally had no lascivious connotation; hence the trademark ankle-length dresses that are commonly worn by the majority of Micronesian women. The majority of Yapese, on the other hand, still wear their traditional clothing, as it is a requirement in most villages to wear traditional clothing. Western clothes come off in the capital and are exchanged for traditional clothes when going to one's village.

The teaching of the missionaries was designed to neutralize women's collective power in order to subvert the traditional order and political power of the islands to and put it under the influence and control of the missionaries. It did not work on the Yapese because their society is structured differently, in a way that could resist this cultural onslaught.

As for the Palauans, the second most traditional culture in Micronesia, the matriarchal culture is fully intact. This may be because they managed to, like African descendents in Cuba, create a syncretistic religion in which the traditional religion was hidden behind the Christianity they had to practice under the colonial administrations.

Women set the tone of the society, because they are the primary nurturers. Whether they teach their young to be predators, prey, or something in between, outside influences that subvert the power and influence of women subvert the integrity of the society as a whole. Modern day "women's power" is often times unsustainable patriarchal power practiced by women, and perpetuated by women who sit in seats of power that substantiate this same power.

In Greek mythology, Athena born from her father Zeus' head, sent Perseus to end the age of matriarchal power and the power of the divine feminine through the taking of Medusa's head. Though Athena was female, her governing orientation was that of a strict patriarchy; that of her father. In the Greek myth, the end of Medusa was the end of the age of the self-defining woman who lived in true partnership with the men in their lives, not subservient to them struggling to place a female face on a male worldview. In Yap, patriarchy can be sustainable; but in Yap, like the rest of Micronesia women control the land, therefore control the allocation of resources, so they are in a position of parity regardless of whose hereditary line is followed. Like all other animal species, there are no "weak females", this is a mental construction created by some human cultures.

It is through the maintenance of traditional women's power that Micronesia will stay alive.

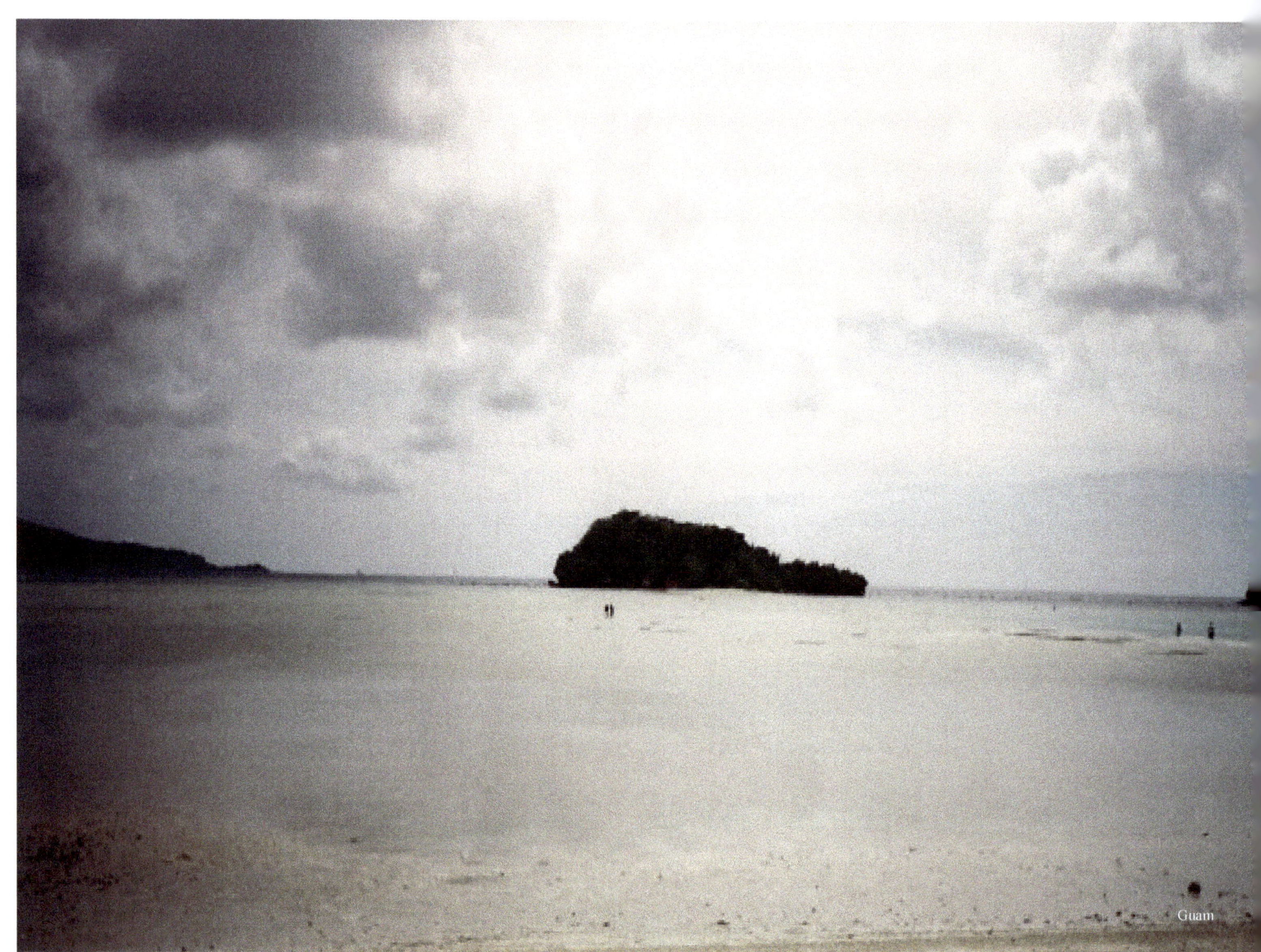
Guam

NO JUSTICE, PEACE

In contemplating the lessons that can be learned from Micronesians, one came to the forefront of my mind – the application of the practice of restorative justice. In Micronesian societies, the integrity of the community is paramount. The needs of the society are balanced with those of the individual. In discussing restorative justice I wish to mention examples of how it is practiced in two places: Palau and Chuuk.

In Palau, when someone commits a crime against the society serious enough that they need to time away from society to contemplate their actions, they are incarcerated. While incarcerated the person is taught skills that will enable them to re-enter the society as a full member once released. Besides being trained in the importance of their role in preserving and maintaining the integrity of the society, two very valued industrial skills in Palau that are taught in prison are: woodblock carving and jewelry making with turtleshell.

In Palau, when someone commits a crime, the whole family is not to be punished, as in the usual case with punitive justice. And the offender at some point will reenter society, and will need to do so as a whole person capable of being a productive citizen. The purpose of punitive justice is to punish the individual for the crime committed. The purpose of restorative justice is to restore the harmony of the community. In administering restorative justice the victim of the crime is not only the person considered offended, but also the society. So healing must occur for all. If an inmate is imprisoned and their family becomes impoverished because they cannot make a living, greater damage to the community is caused. The person is incarcerated so the affront to the offended parties' is acknowledged and corrective measures are taken. While this person is incarcerated, he can develop skills so that he can earn a living selling the crafts he creates so that money can go to his family. In this way, when he gets out of prison, he has had time to reorient himself to the importance of living in the community as a valuable and productive member of the society; his family maintains its integrity; and he can use these new skills to generate an income for his family, an income that he was likely not able to make before going to prison; and he now is in the position to apprentice younger people in the skills that he had learned. In this way harmony is restored to the community as a whole.

In Chuuk, before this increasing substitution of traditional justice with American justice that comes with being a Freely Associated State of the U.S., the Chuukese style of justice was to restore the integrity of community as quickly as possible. For example, if one man kills another man, the punishment for this crime and that the killer's family would have to pay large amount of restitution to the offended family, i.e. breadfruit, taro, rice, fish, etc.; and then the offending family would lose their son to the family that was offended. He was to then take the place of the son that he took from this other family. In learning to now love him as their son, forgiveness is cultivated and community is restored.

The Micronesian sense of justice is one in which love – the community – is reestablished in the administration of justice. In this way, where there is peace is the result of justice.

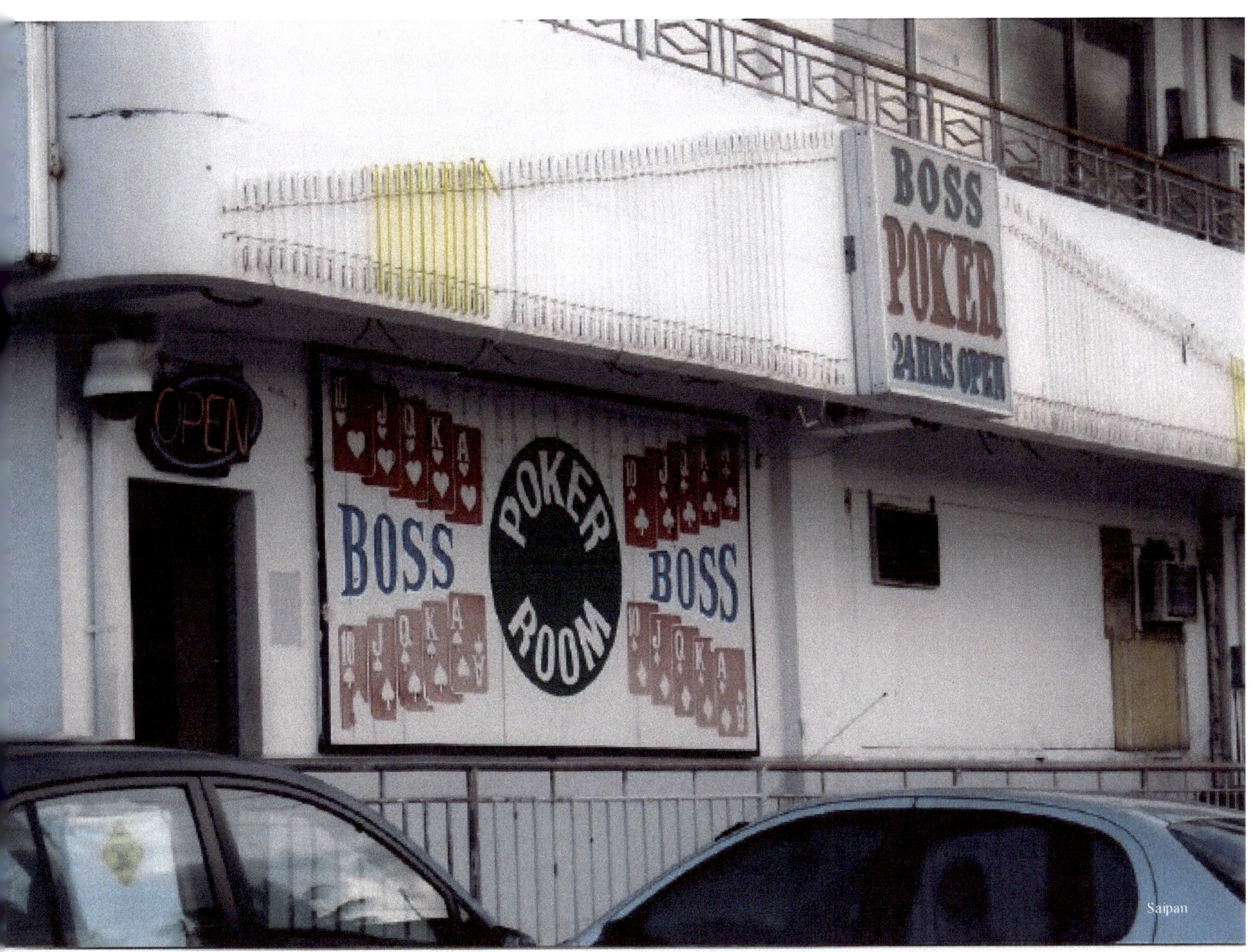

OPEN
BOSS
POKER
ROOM
BOSS
BOSS
POKER
24HRS OPEN
Saipan

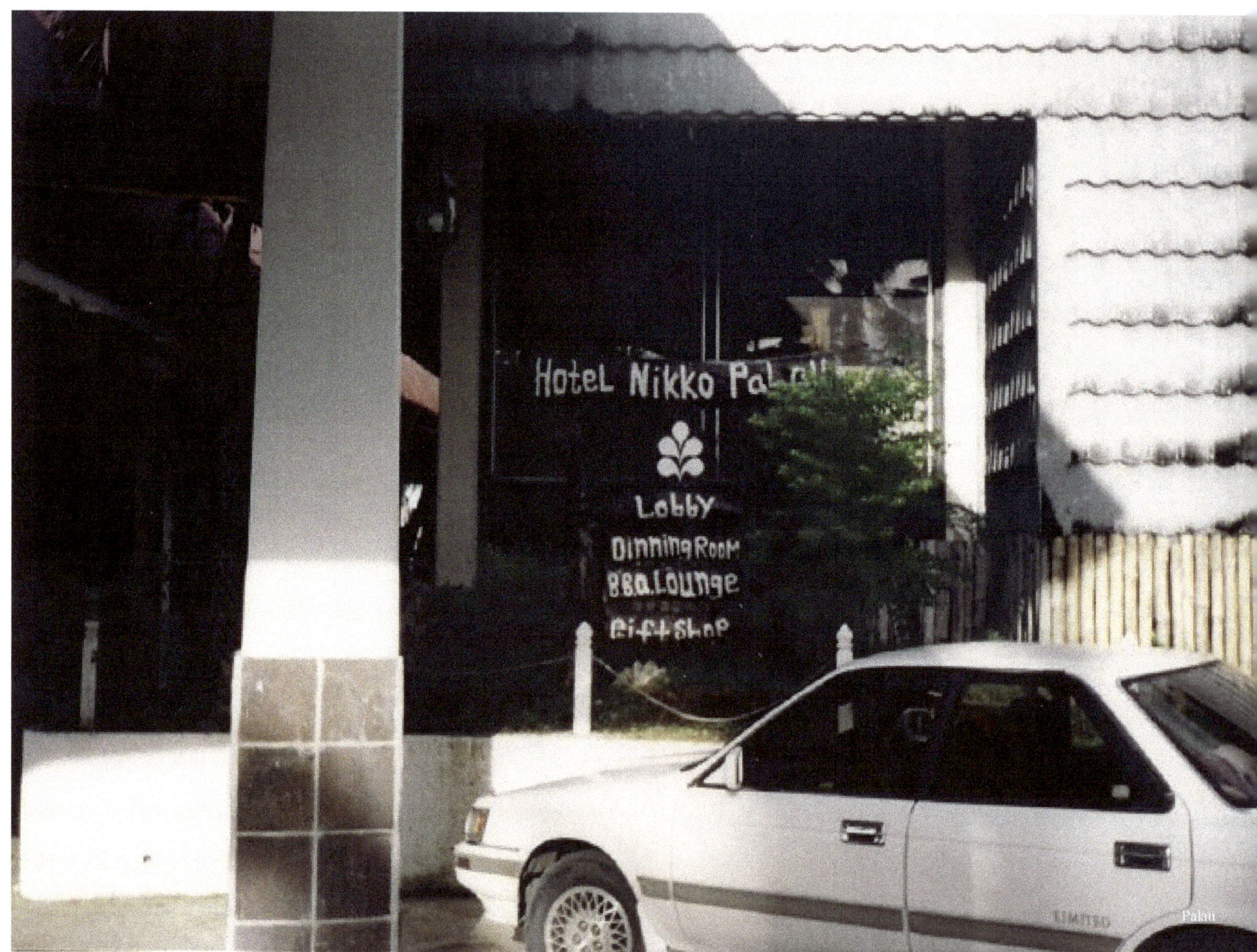
Hotel Nikko Pala
Lobby
Dinning Room
BBq Lounge
Gift Shop
Palau

THE OUTSIDE COMES IN

The traveler was "island-hopping", taking a plane route that takes passengers between Guam and Honolulu and to every stop between the two: Guam - Chuuk - Pohnpei - Kosrae - Kwajalein - Majuro - Honolulu. From Guam to Majuro, seated beside me was a senior official in the Kosraean government who had been in high position ever since the FSM was granted independence in the transition from the being part of the Trust Territory of the Pacific Islands to the Federated States of Micronesia. He shared with me some thoughts that he had about decisions that were made in government years ago. One of which, was the decision to open the airport on Kosrae and the other, to allow cable television. I wouldn't say that he was speaking with a feeling of regret, but rather, a desire to have had more information in regard to the potentialities that could arise when that degree of access to the outside world happens too quickly.

As opposed to the interaction that comes with other modes of transportation and mass communication, the age of the jet airplane and worldwide television broadcasts add a degree of complexity to the equation that government decision-makers may not have been able to contemplate. Both of these move so fast, and with such intensity that the natural transitions that occur between people and places on trains, ships, cars, and radio cannot occur.

The medium of radio connects people but there is always an awareness that it is being broadcasted from "somewhere else" and by "somebody," that embodies the worldview of the place from where it is being broadcast. With this as a functioning reality, one is in a better position to think critically about the content and determine the acceptability of this content to one's environment. For the radio broadcast, there is an understanding that the broadcast is made to persons who may or may not share their views.

A traveler can watch China slowly turn into Russia riding the Trans-Siberian and Trans-Siberian Railway; and West turn into East on the Orient Express, and vice-versa. Travel by ship or train is slow enough that one can see the transformation of the people and places into other people and places therefore a natural realization of the existence of a different reality, a different worldview us more apparent to a traveler. The jet age however, allowed for the emergence of the "tourist", one without the concerted effort to contemplate one's self in reflection to one's surroundings. It became easier to unconsciously and consciously carry a desire to experience one's own world in someone else's environment.

In speaking to the gentleman, it appeared that in the attempt to "let-in the modern world" to increase "opportunities and freedom" for the people, the opposite occurred. It actually took away their freedom. As opposed to the present reality of an economic motivation for every human activity, before "contact", the human experience was a very multifaceted experience.

Without prior awareness on how to mitigate the potential negative affects of allowing products from the outside to come into the socioeconomic milieu of Kosrae, and without the corresponding ability to acquire them, it turned them (the people) and their land and ocean resources into sellable commodities. There was no predominate preexisting cash economy on Kosrae to support the newly important material needs that now exist on the island.

The decision to allow cable television also had an unseen effect; it constantly reinforced the need for material items even though there is no adequate means of acquiring them. This new value system created the necessity for a cash economy in a place where there are few exports outside of limited land and sea resources and remittances from islanders whom have to live abroad in order to send money home. It has become too expensive to live "comfortably" on the island because of the lessening capacity to meet local needs through local industrial efforts, and because the people and resources have to be reallocated in order to acquire these formerly unneeded things.

There was a bicultural dance that was done to maintain solvency of the culture and being Christian (in this 1800s fundamentalist interpretation), that no longer had to be maintained once cable television came into existence on the island. Though there was socio-cultural disruption caused by this incongruent social ideal posed by the missionaries, there still was no real model to emulate on a large scale, because of how the missionary families organized and conducted themselves. But with cable television, "modern womanhood" was now available to all of these young women and girls who no longer had the benefit of living in a "women's house" and learning how to be women from their elders; the culture of conspicuous consumption and individualistic materialism would become their new teacher. As supposed to being a whole person whose intrinsic value comes from being born and being a member of a family, community, society, their esteem now depended upon one's potential to consume recognized material icons.

For the young men, cable television teaches them how inadequate they are as men. What is defined as manhood on television is that manhood is based on one's ability to consume. "Poverty" becomes a reality when local skills no longer have any value in the society. In this modern era, opportunities in the cash economy are far and in between, while at the same time local skills such as fishing, weaving, carving, net making, and traditional navigating have increasingly little or no value in the modern society. From the perspective of self-esteem needs, mastery of one's craft gave a lot of men an internal self of worth and relevance. In the modern day, the skills that were taught to boys in the transition to manhood have little importance and often can not translate into cash generating activities, therefore many men no longer have purpose. The material goods presented on the television far exceed the capacity of the local people's ability to obtain them. All this does is breed frustration, because the television is finishing the transition from children to adulthood, as well as instilling a feeling of inadequacy in all youth. This creates a transition into adulthood in which one's actions can either lead to the greater ability to live the "Good Life", as defined by the television, or the "bad life", a continuation of the status quo. In this new worldview, the mastery of local skills and the adherence to custom are often viewed as obstacles and hindrances to obtaining the "Good Life". The ability or inability to consume the material icons presented on the television set defines whether he is a man or not, rather then through. Powerlessness from these feelings of inadequacy can manifest as self-destructive behavior taken out on himself and his family.

Because manhood and womanhood are defined in this media, romantic relationships are a major component of this social training. As opposed to the past where one's unconditional love needs where met by being a member of a family, village, or clan; because the integrity of their social bonds is being weakened by this outsides forces, the "security" of this love is also threatened. With a weakening relationship to the providers of unconditional love in one's life, as taught on television, all of one's love needs can be found in one person. For older Micronesians, this concept may seem totally crazy, but to the youth whom are being raised into adulthood by the television set, this makes perfect sense. So, these youth grow up considerably more instable than their elders, because meeting one's love/belonging needs (as well as other internal needs) is placed into a dice throw of hoping that some other person can provide external answers (their romantic relationship) to internal questions (the need for a sense of belonging and interconnectedness with all things). Happiness, rather than being a state of being, becomes contingent upon the success of one's romantic relationships and the possession of material things. The anxiety that this kind of externalization of happiness and self brings on a society, as you can imagine, brings in an X-factor than noone in the society has any experience dealing with.

In the present era, suicide has become an epidemic among Micronesian youth. A youth will take their life over a relationship gone bad. As opposed to the past where one's self integrity was indwelling and the sharing of one's gifts and talents with the community formed the basis of one's personal psychology; everything is now externalized, including one's sense of identity. The chaos and uncertainty of an externalized sense of self brings the likelihood that the random changes that life brings can actually shatters one's internal world. One's internal stability is affected by the new sense of time presented in the media as well. Life is no longer based on indigenous time, circular time, time based on natural processes, but rather manufactured time, in this case, linear time. Circular time reemphasizes the impermanence of all things and the need to cultivate resilience in order to maintain harmony with the universe, while linear time projects an idea of the permanence of structures despite the law of causality and the certainty of change. For a person new to linear worldview and possessing an externalized sense of self, life can be overwhelming; and the only way to escape the "permanent reality" of their lives is to leave life itself. Many of the larger Micronesian islands have youth suicide rates far exceeded those one would find in the U.S.

It is an interesting irony is that the dispersion of global modern culture based on consumption is thought to be necessary for development and progress; but the reality is that is does the opposite. The sharing of culture is a good thing. It is like cross-pollenization; but the danger comes when the process is so fast and so powerful that there is no exchange. When one party believes that its way is "universal" to all humans and the receiver is so awed by the delivery system in which this culture is presented, the maintenance of the receiver's own cultural integrity diminished in importance. Nature abhors monocultures - they diminish a species' ability to be resilient. The "universal culture" brought to Micronesia is monoculture.

A question: What was the impetus behind the large scale migration of Irish people to the US? – in scientific terms, because nature abhors monocultures; in sociological terms, because of the Irish Potato Famine. How did this come about? It came about because of the English colonization of Ireland. It was desirous that Ireland would serve as the breadbasket of Great Britain and that all arable lands would be use to grow agriculture. The crop of choice was potatoes. The scientists of the time had the idea that one single "super breed" of potatoes would produce the greatest yield, therefore meet the production objectives of the colony. The problem – one single breed may have shared strength, but also has the same weaknesses. In this case, there was a potato disease called Potato Blight. It infected the crops and spread like wildfire because there was no resistance to; resistance was bred out in the process of creating one single culture of potatoes. Subsequently, the population starved, causing a mass exodus to the U.S. in hopes of creating a life with food.

Human diversity is not important because it is a nice, warm, fuzzy feeling term; it is a ecological necessity that applies to humans as much as it applies to plants and animals. The most important trait in a species is resiliency, i.e. at the end of the day; the only thing that matters to the perpetuation of human societies is their ability to respond favorably to the X-factor, unplanned crises. Monocultures may appear to be strong because the concentration of a common strength that they possess, but they are also extremely vulnerable because of their common weaknesses. A variety of traits in a society allows it to be able to access an abundance of solutions to problems that it would not have if differences were not cultivated and appreciated. Just to reiterate this, I will state it in technical terms – there are static and dynamic systems –static systems have short term success over dynamic systems, but always fail dues to their lack of flexibility.

The realization of individual creative potential, a virtue in Micronesian cultures, is the only glue that truly binds people to each other, both in individual relationships as well as between distinct cultural groups and the greater blended societies that they compare. It is this mosaic, not melting pot, that provides the essential traits of resiliency that a society must have if it is able to survive unexpected crises. Those societies who cannot, go extinct whether through absorption into a society with true or projected cultural integrity, or just die because they can no longer thrive in their own environment. Nature is pretty oblivious to soliciting reasons to why resiliency is not promoted; either a group is or isn't, and thrives or dies. This is why humans have to align their endeavors with the natural reality that they live in. Any long running human society that still exists in 2009 has been doing something right in order to survive this long. We should honor and acknowledge this; to not do so is to welcome extinction for everyone. For the groups that we allow to be assimilated into a "universal global culture" are possibly the holders of knowledge that only they have, that we will all need in a time or crisis. It is paramount to the long-term sustainability of any human society to maintain the cultural integrity of all human groups. None is greater or of more importance than another; to do so is to go the way of all of the societies whom no longer exist and many of whom even their names no longer reside in the minds of people.

Some thoughts to ponder: I ask you to consider, even if it is based solely on the feeling of self-preservation and not the on the appreciation of the beauty of human creative expression, the importance of cultivating your own creative potential and sharing it with the world and assisting however you can in the individual creative potential based on congruence with their higher selves. If we cease to attempt answering internal questions with external answers, the world may be a much better place.

Micronesia is one of few places in the world left that has not been totally absorbed into the global consumer culture. For this reason, it is of great importance to the human family as a whole that the diversity that still exists in the hearts and minds of people of these islands in maintained. Micronesia is one of the few places in the world where people, today, can live fully sustainable, productive, happy, fulfilled lives without the need for factory produced goods. Despite the challenges places on their cultures by outsiders, they still live in communal societies in which children are not viewed as "responsibilities" or "consequences", but truly as gifts whom people vie to raise even other people's children even before there are born; and places where you can walk up to any person you see as a matter of course and say "I'm hungry" and they will take their house and feed you.

The societies of Micronesia are based on love and shared survival.

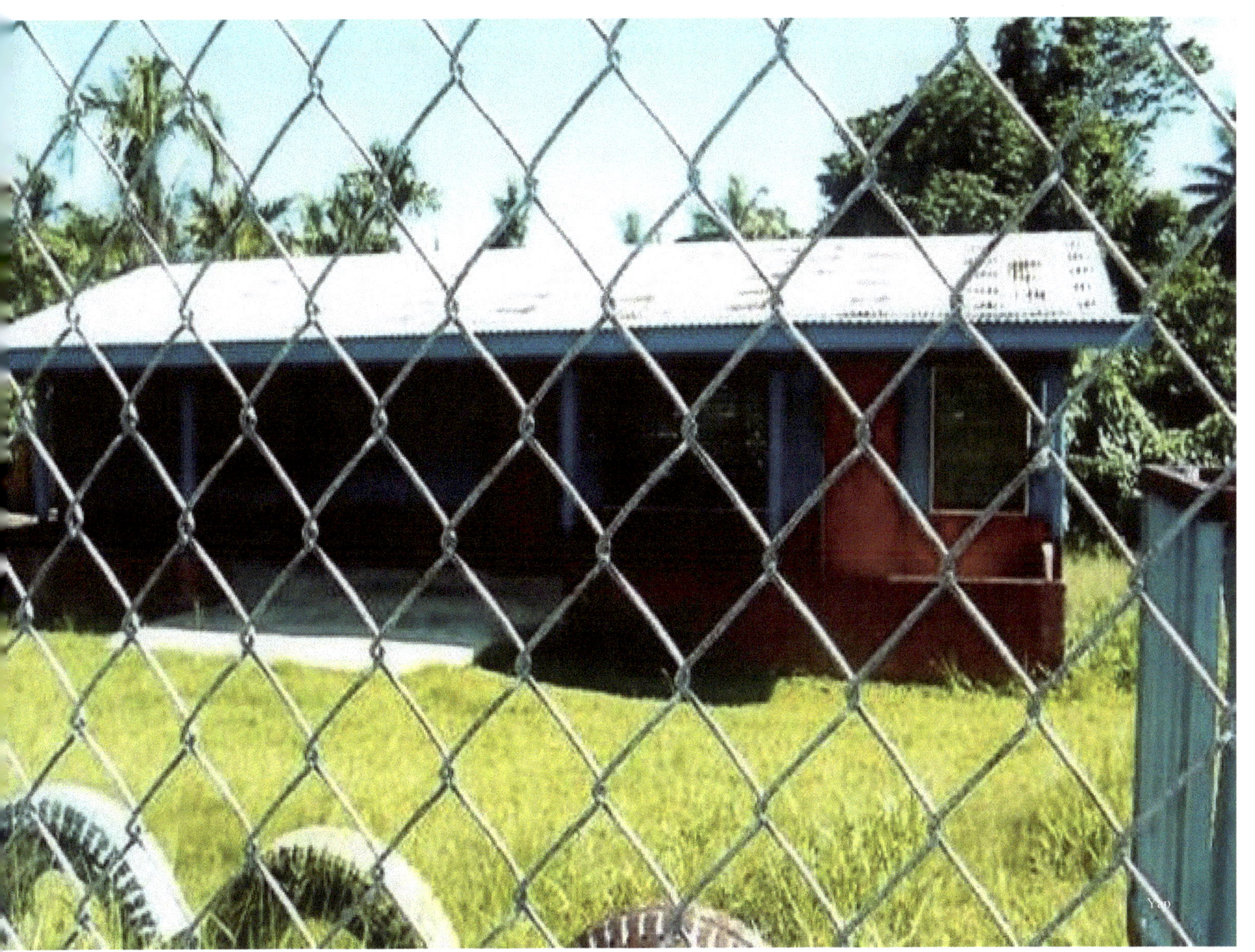
Yap

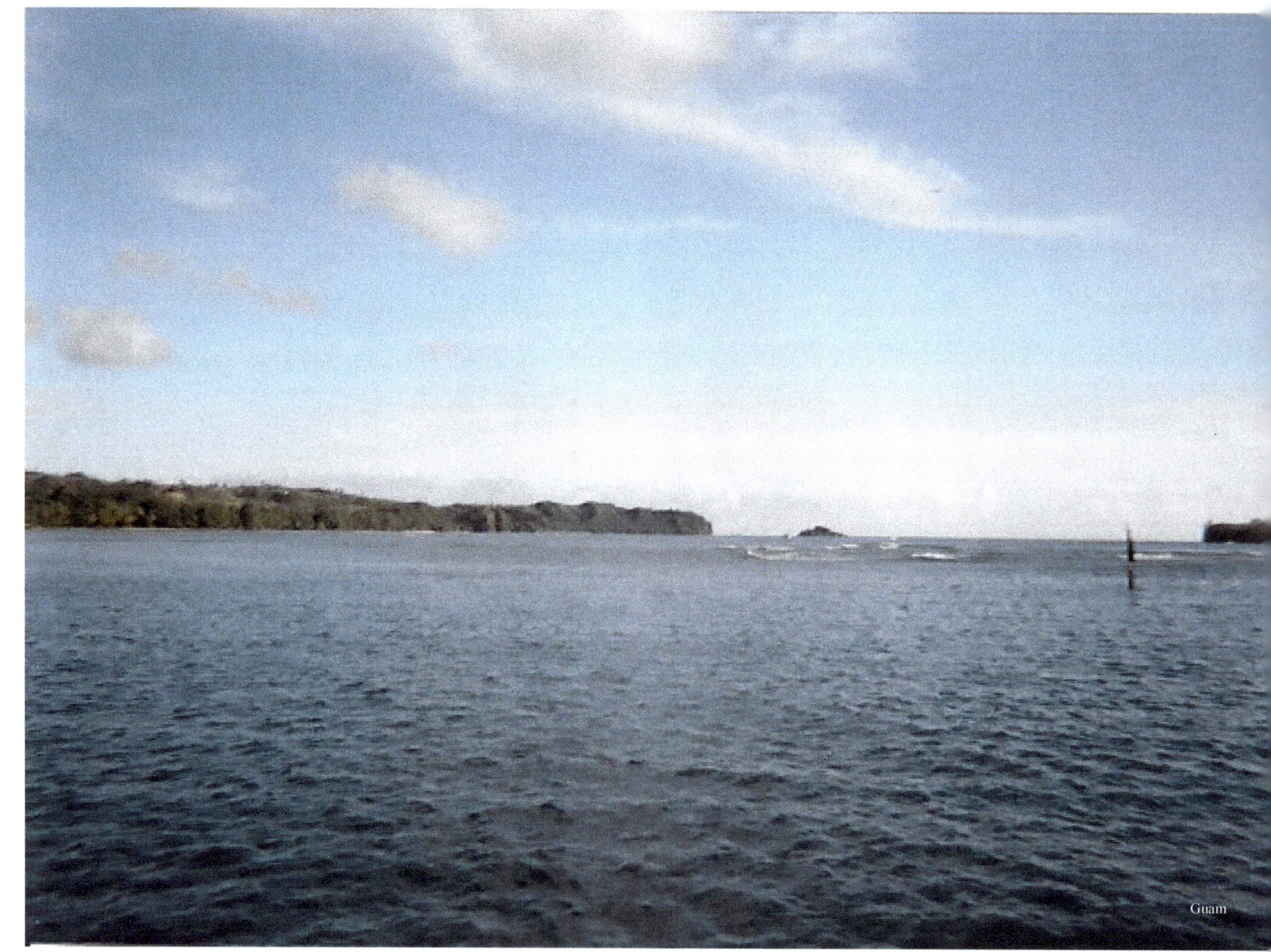

Guam

PREPARING THE PACIFIC CHILD

For twenty-six years, educators from the Western Pacific islands have convened the Pacific Educational Conference. In 2009, the conference was held in Guam and the participants explored the meaning of and effective approaches for "preparing the Pacific child for life".

The question "for what type of life" begs to be asked and answered. Should the Pacific child continue to become cannon fodder in wars in faraway lands? Should she be prepared to do mindless work in the low paying service industry? Should he be prepared to immigrate to the U.S. mainland in search of employment in a chicken factory? When the life options of many children from the Pacific Islands, principally Micronesia, are considered, one must lament the dismal future that lies ahead for most of these children.

Statistics indicate that the lives of too many Micronesian children in particular are in shambles. What represented the lives of these children before and after the U.S. colonization after WWII is one of stark contrast. These islands are now engulfed in a wave of change spawned by Western values that is creating social disruption in these traditional societies. These changes are drastically affecting the well-being and changing the life chances for children from these islands.

Prior to U.S. colonialism, families were strong and the extended family played a significant role in the lives of children. Traditionally, a high value was placed on children. Children were loved, cherished, and cared for by all members of the family which included grandparents, aunts, uncles, and older siblings. Responsibilities for the care and guidance of children were shared. Children were taught clear roles and rules for behavior, including the value of respecting elders who represented authority and protection.

With U.S. colonialism, came the destruction of the traditional way of life of people in Micronesia. Traditions broke down and the people began to experience "a crisis of values". Children, the most vulnerable of group would ultimately suffer most. The safe and secure lives that children from the Pacific Islands once enjoyed are no more. Now due to being forced into a dollar economy Micronesians are emigrating out of their home islands. As a result, nuclear families are being established by young people who without the knowledge and support of other family members have complete responsibility for caring for and guiding their children. Divorce rates are high and domestic abuse is epidemic. Now confusion in values results in discipline is often permissive or non-existent.

Previously unheard of social problems now menace children from Micronesia. There are high numbers of teen pregnancies; a high incidence of alcohol and drug abuse, and suicide rates among young people. Most disturbing, children once so highly valued in Micronesian societies are being abused. Increasingly there are high numbers of children being neglected and maltreated.

There appears to be one and only one solution to heal this condition and to repair the broken lives of Micronesian children; a return to traditional Micronesian cultural values. Repeatedly, Micronesian educators presented papers which spoke of efforts to save their children by reclaiming and restoring traditional values. Educators from Palau spoke about "cultural lessons for life success" and those from the Republic of the Marshall Islands shared ways in which "Marshallese" skills, knowledge, and values were needed in an effort to "Majolize" the curriculum that Marshallese students studied.

Micronesia represents the good life for many who visit or have immigrated there, but for the children of indigenous Micronesians, life is anything but good. Unless, drastic measures are taken and soon to return Micronesian children to their "true culture", life on their islands will be paradise for everyone but them. The very next you visit the islands and you see the picture of a young Micronesian man fallen in combat in Iraq or Afghanistan in the Guam airport, or read in the local newspaper the story of some Micronesian youth arrested for drug abuse, consider that they were once a proud and prosperous people whose lives were interrupted by outsiders with more powerful weapons.

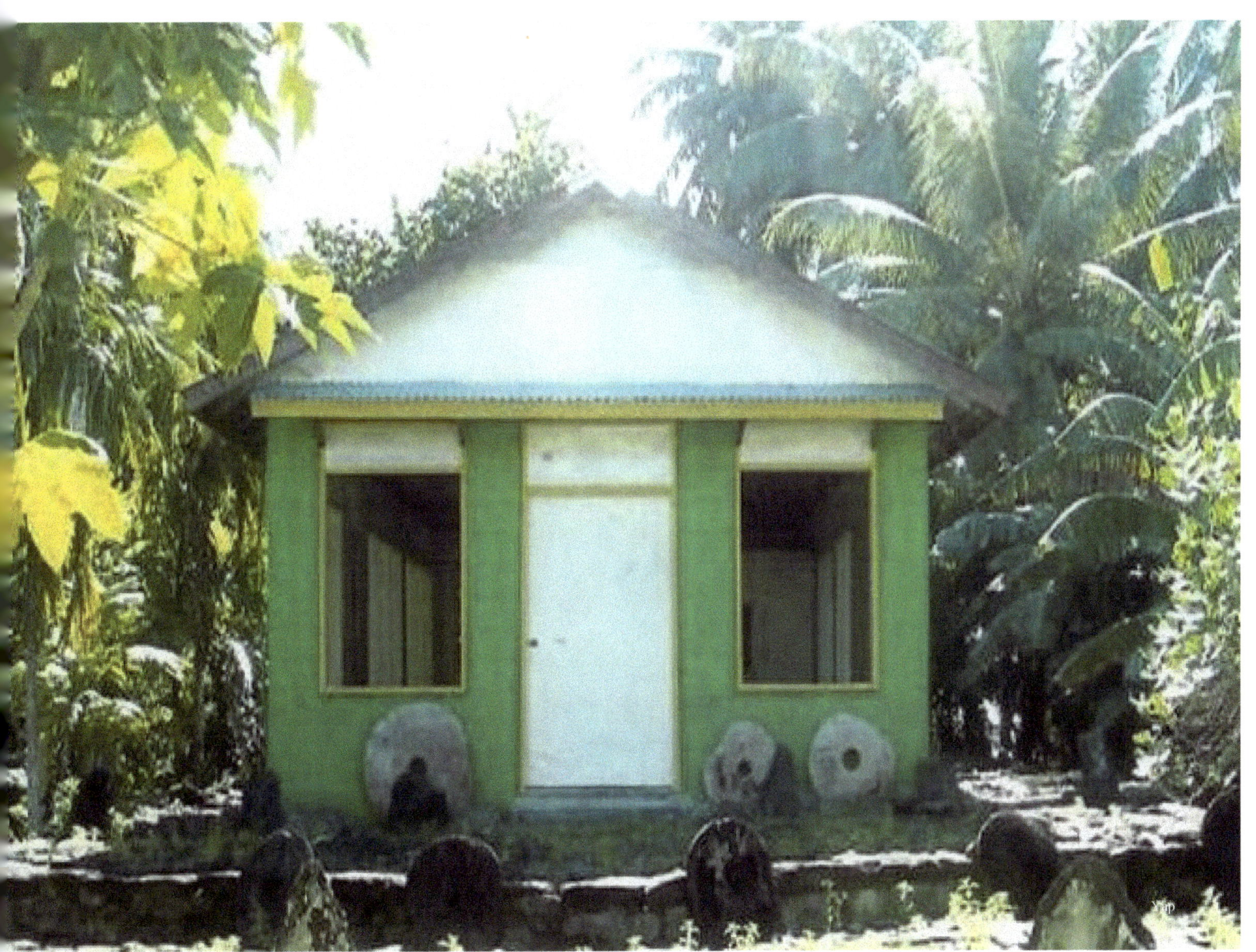

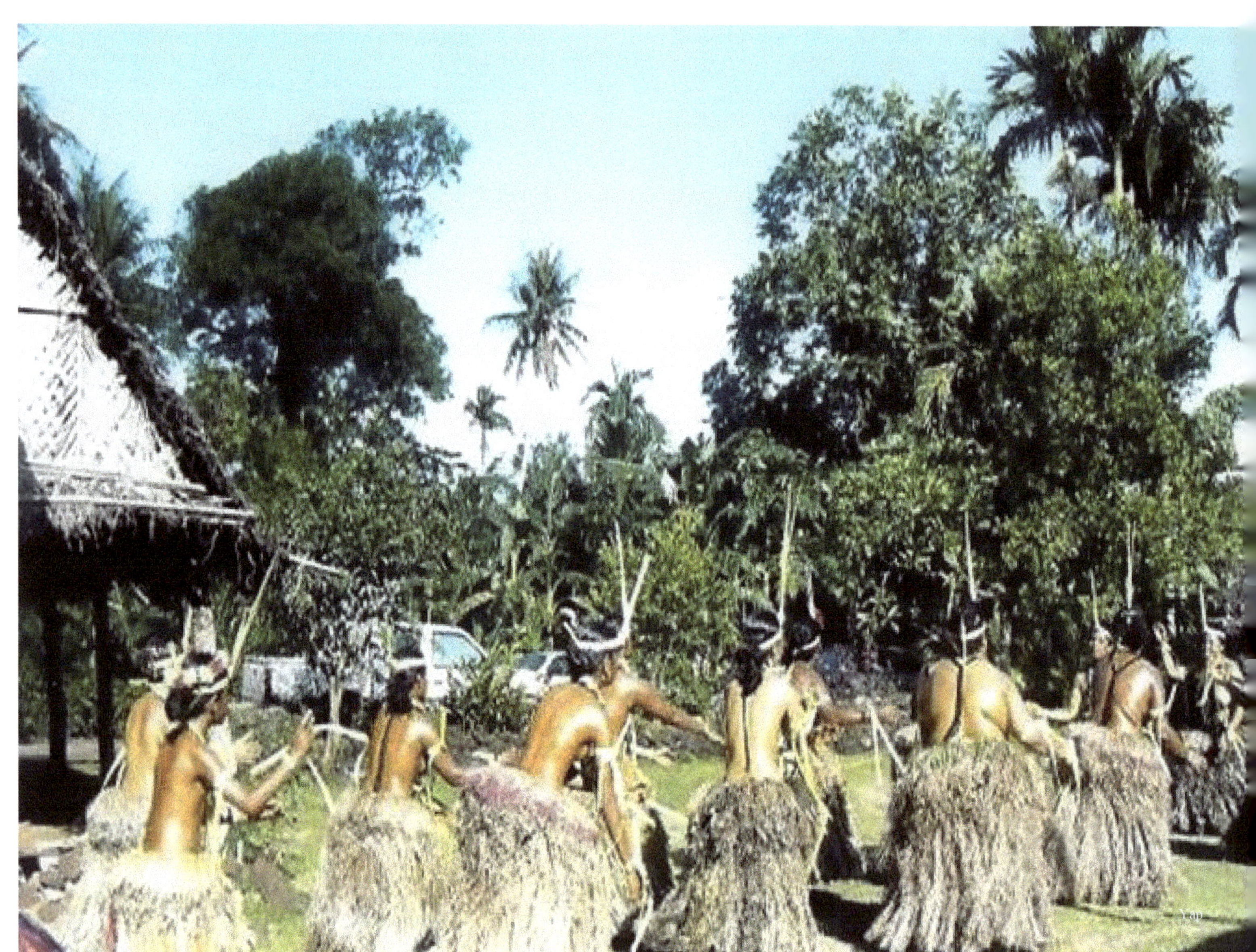

EPILOGUE

Conquest, occupation, colonization, and paternalism have brought many changes to Micronesia. Christianity and westernization have taken a tremendous toll, especially on family life, the loss of a subsistence economy and traditional skills. Micronesians are however, more than ever discovering that progress is not all its supposed to be, that there is value and wisdom in traditional values and customs. They realize that the good life is best measured in stable families, the healthy upbringing of children, freedom from undue stress and social ills, and a general sense of well-being. On these beautiful, tranquil islands, if one chooses, one can still find a sense of peace and well-being that is unmatched.

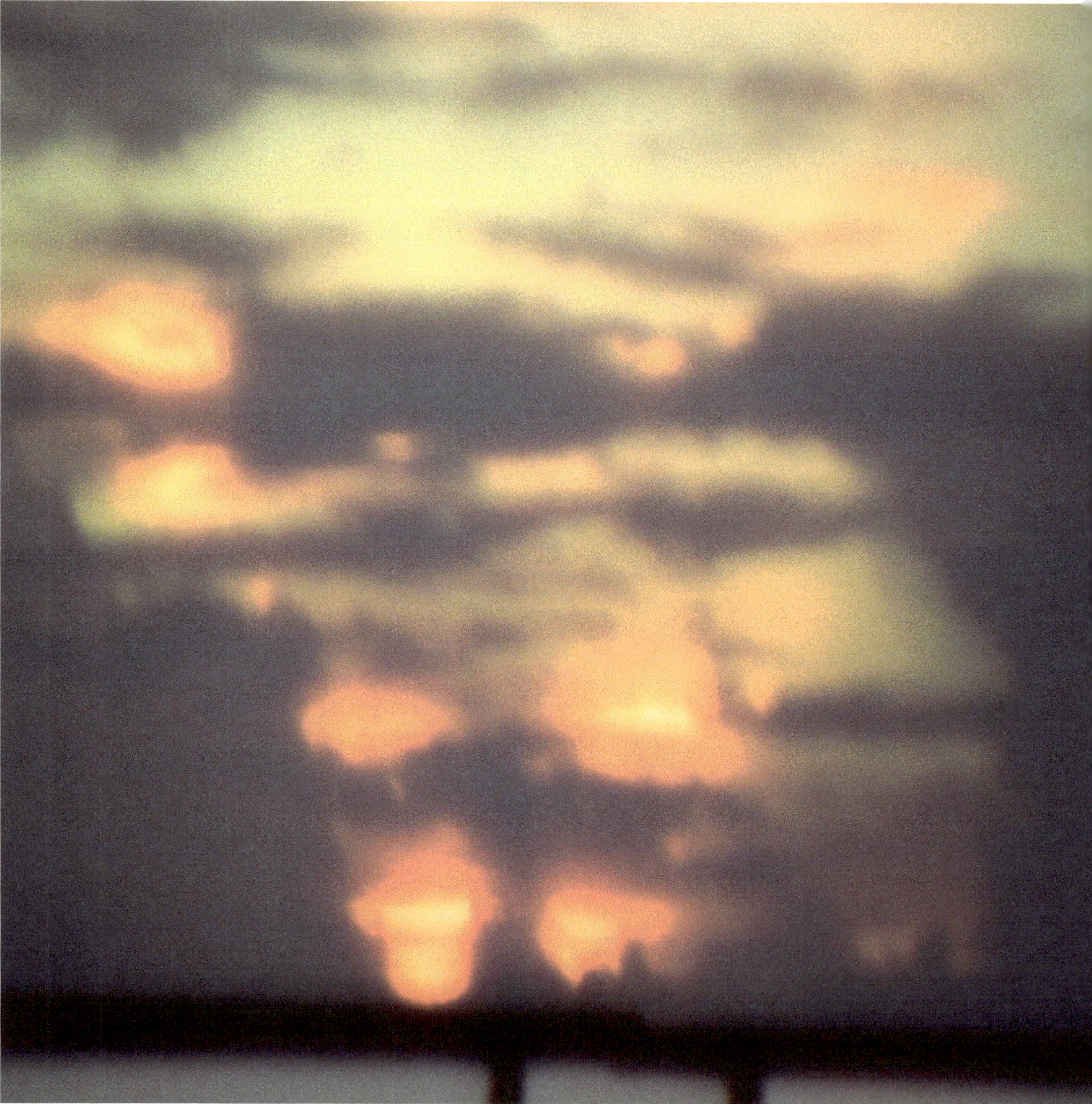

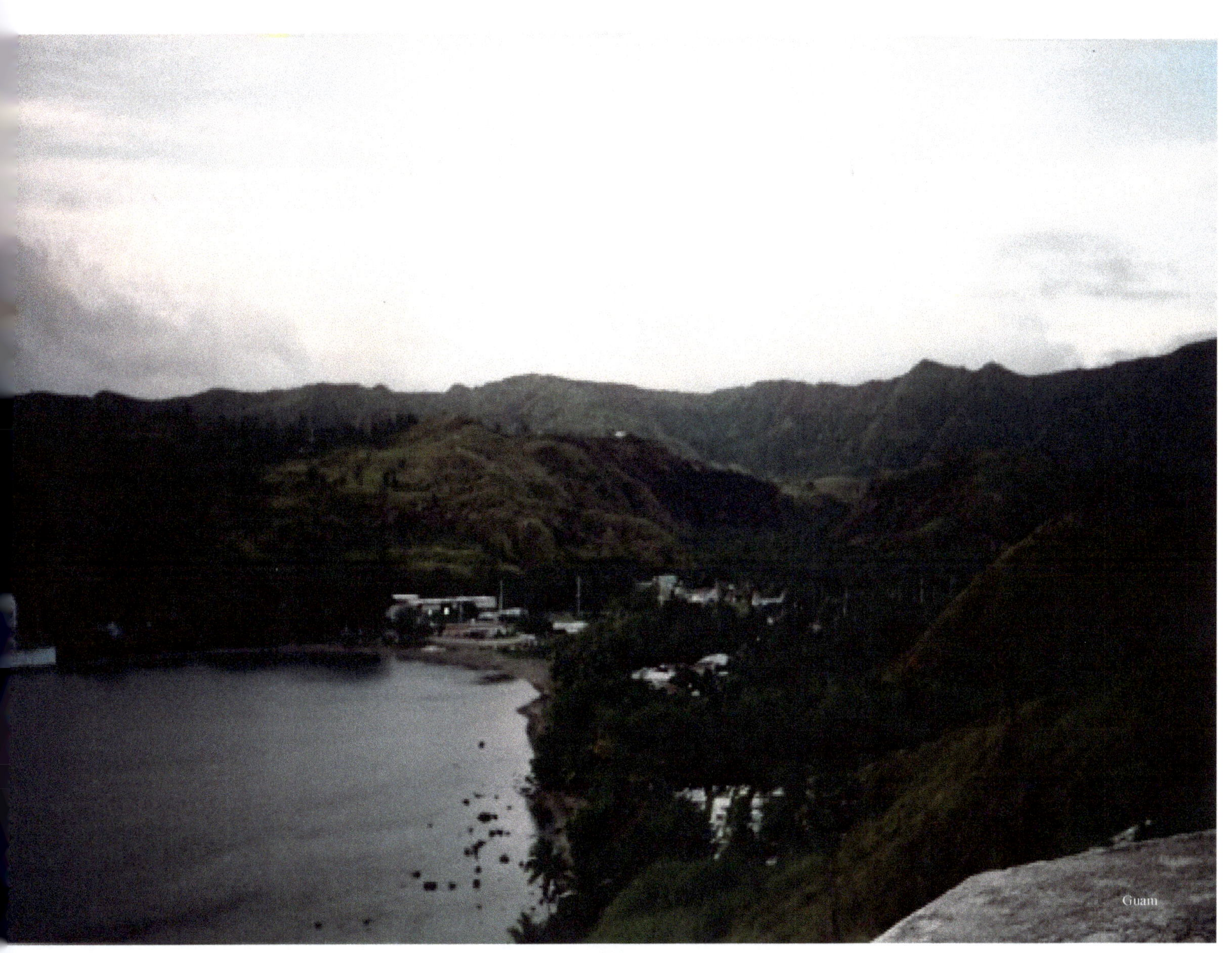
Guam

"Prayer for peace"
We have visited this place many times and communed the souls of you, the bereaved dead. In the event of the fiftieth anniversary of the end of World War II, we would like to express our respect to the memory of all the spirits of Japanese and non Japanese war dead who sleep here.
In order to pray for lasting world peace, we build this monument.
February, 1996
The Chiba Association for the Bereaved Families of the War Dead, Japan

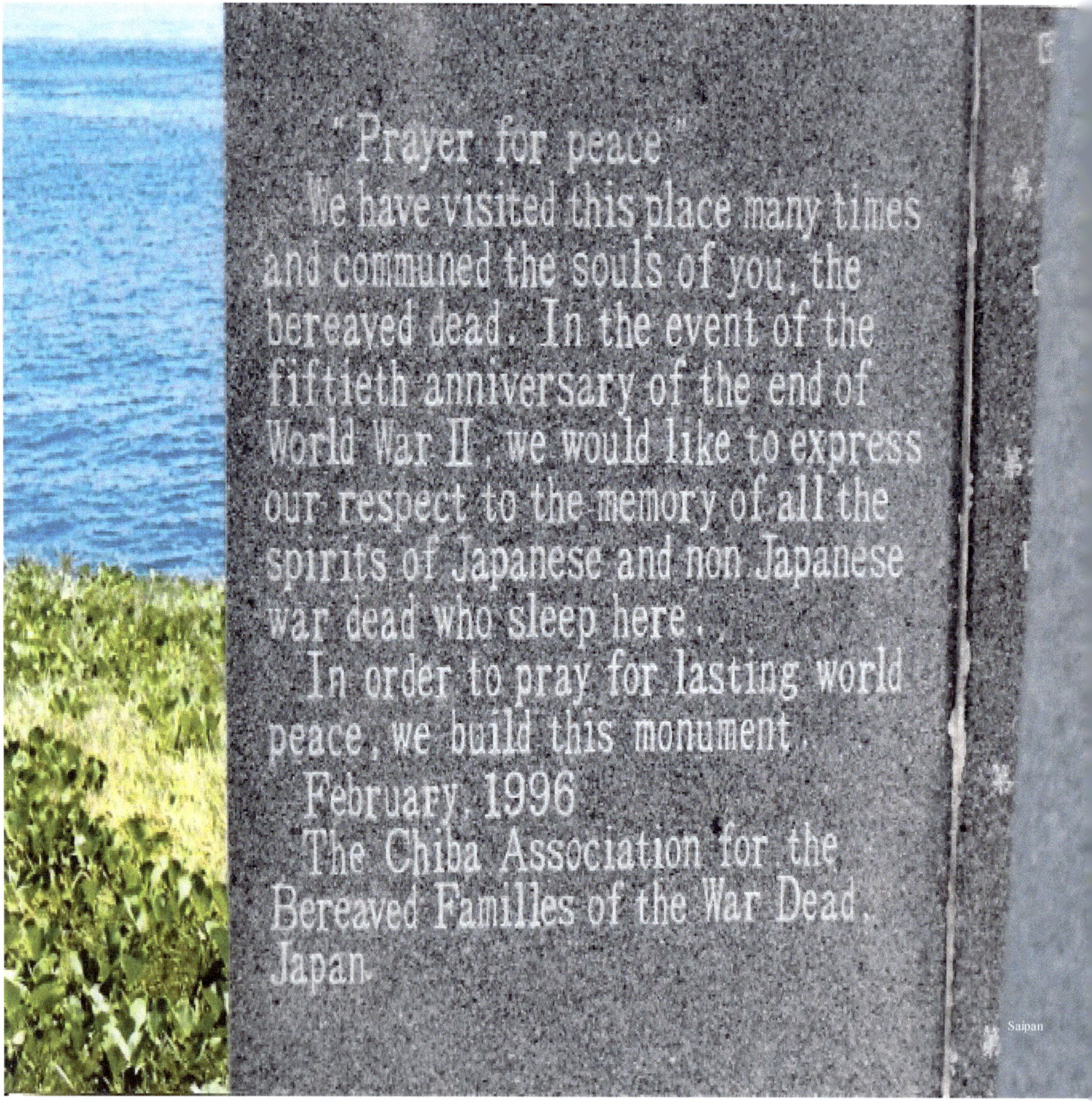

Saipan

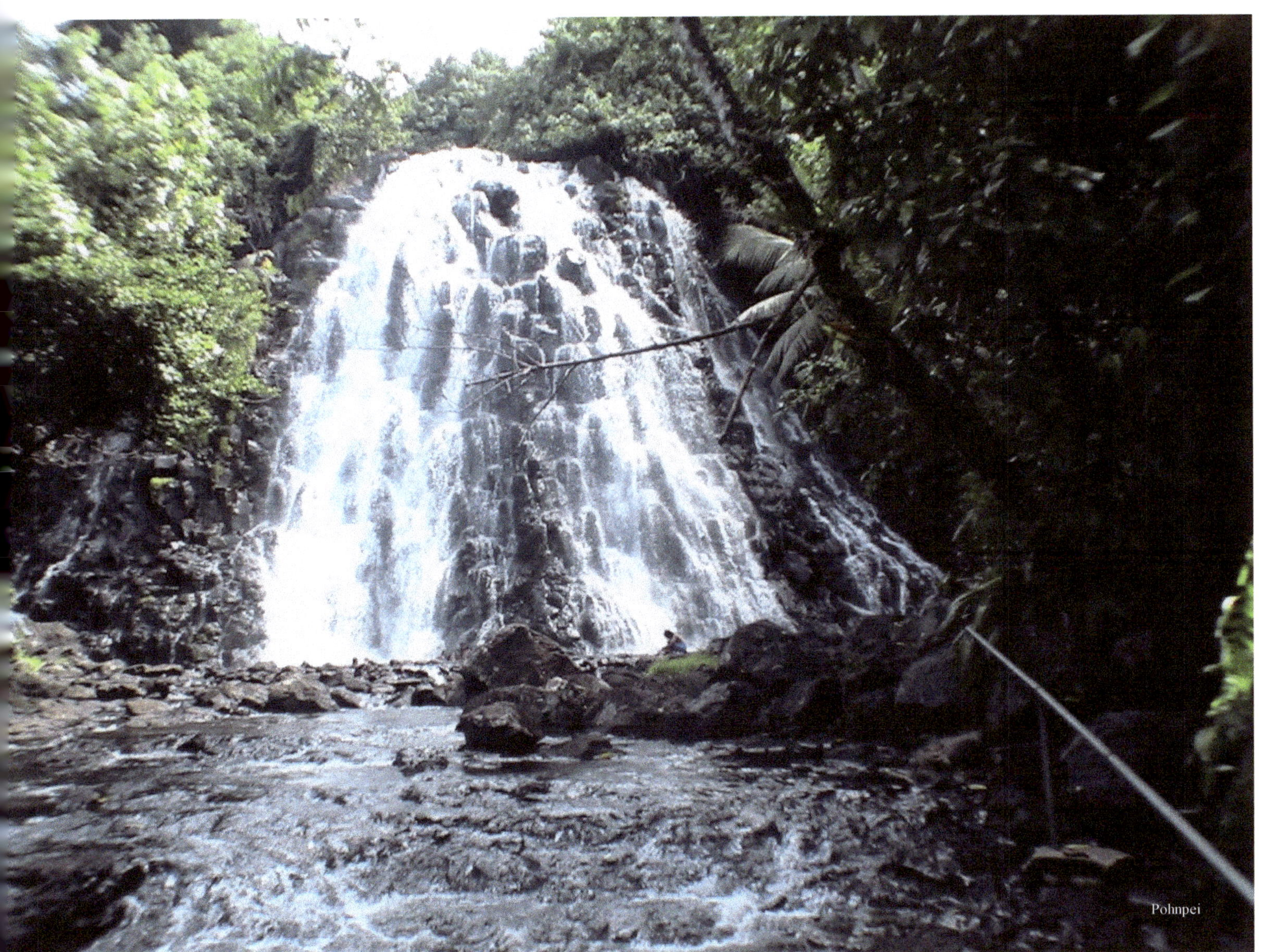

Pohnpei

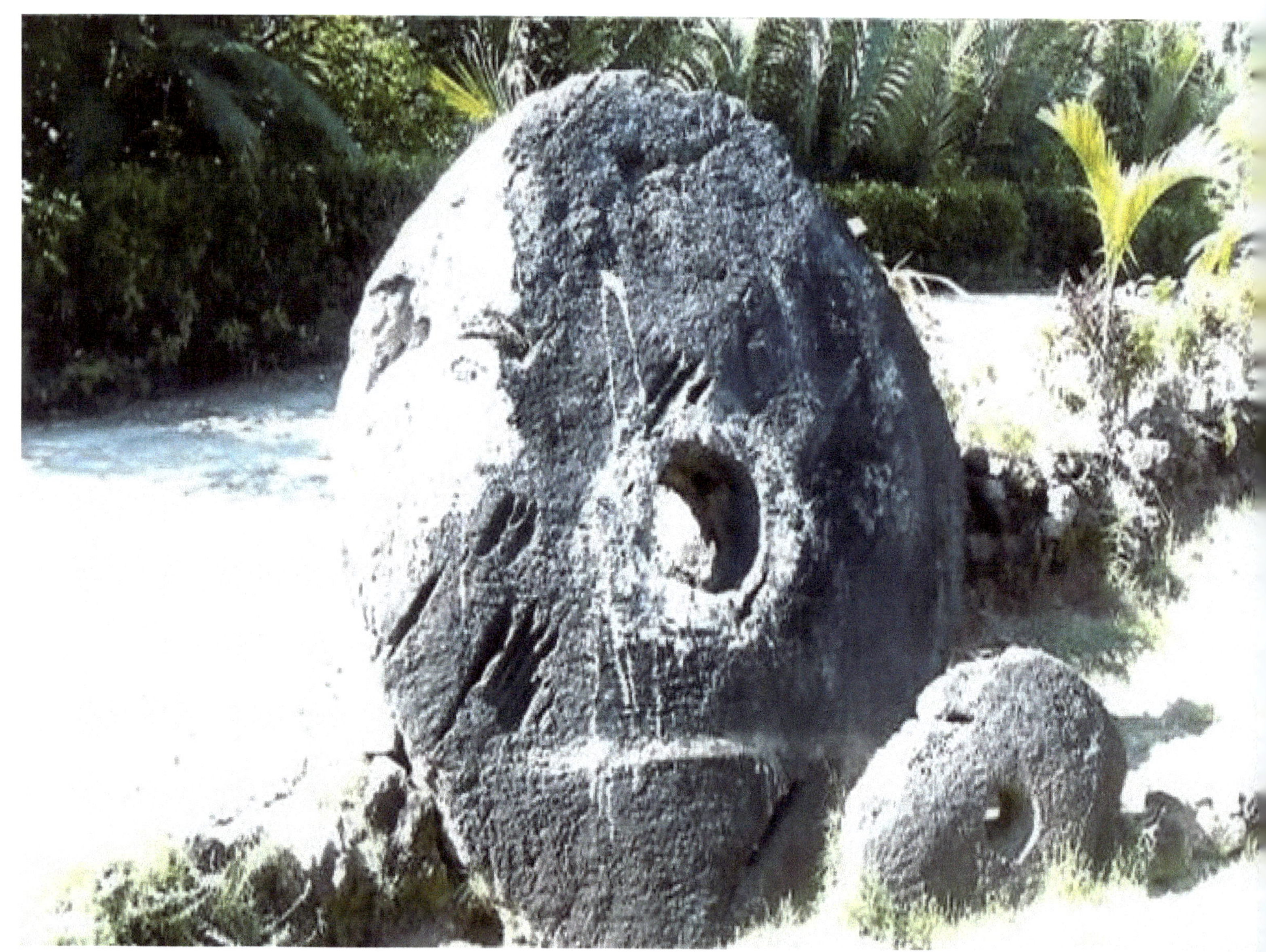

Saipan

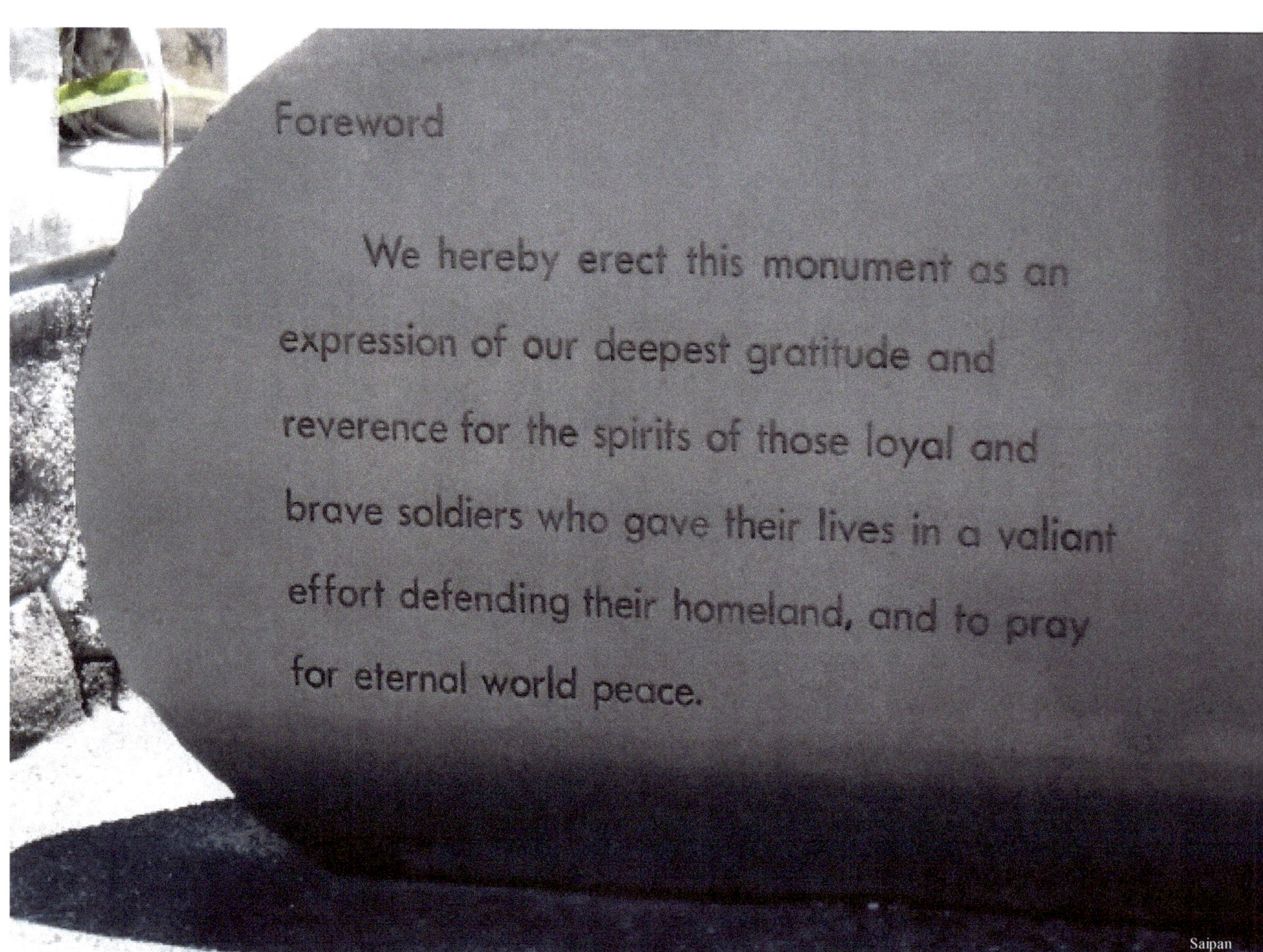

Foreword

We hereby erect this monument as an expression of our deepest gratitude and reverence for the spirits of those loyal and brave soldiers who gave their lives in a valiant effort defending their homeland, and to pray for eternal world peace.

Saipan

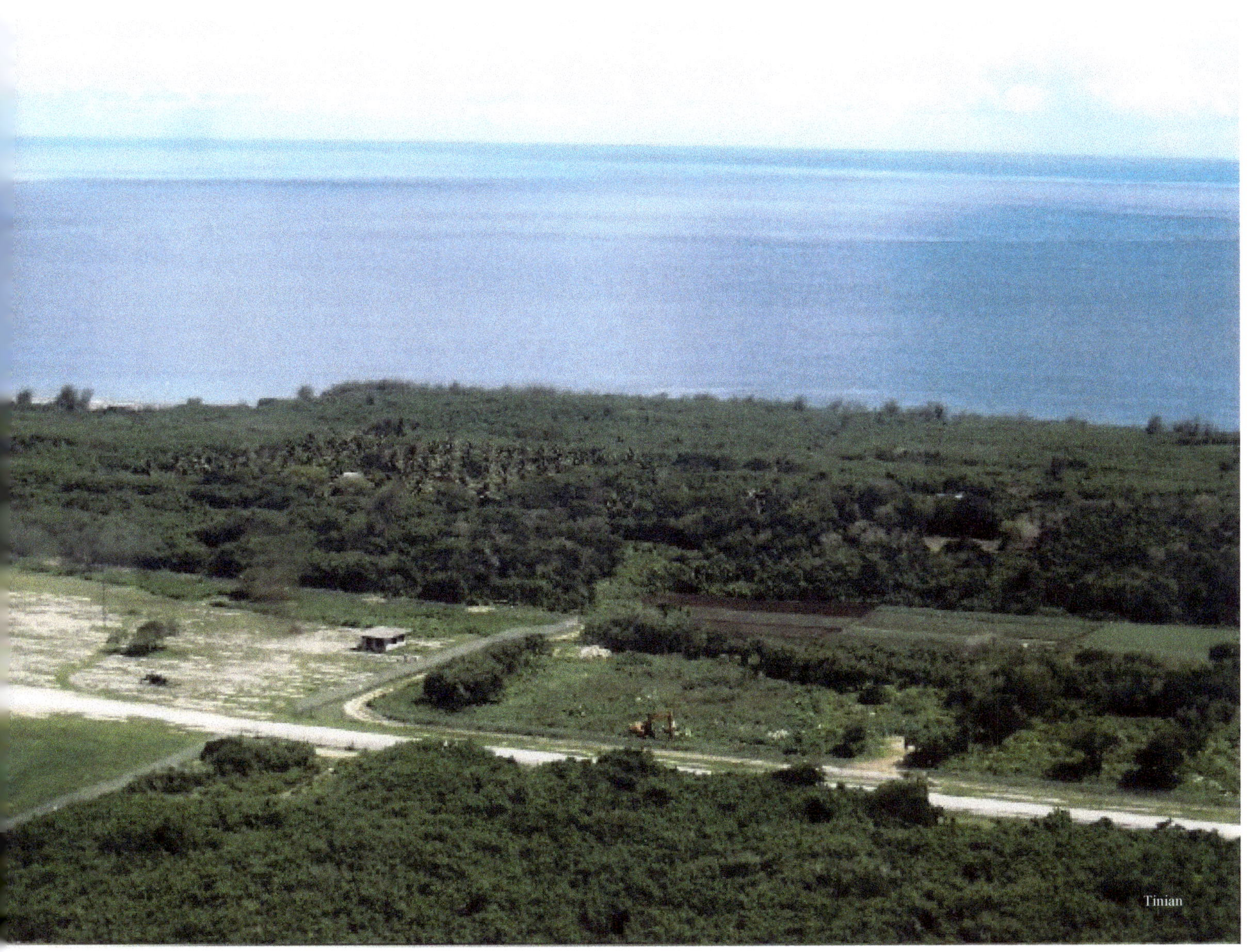
Tinian

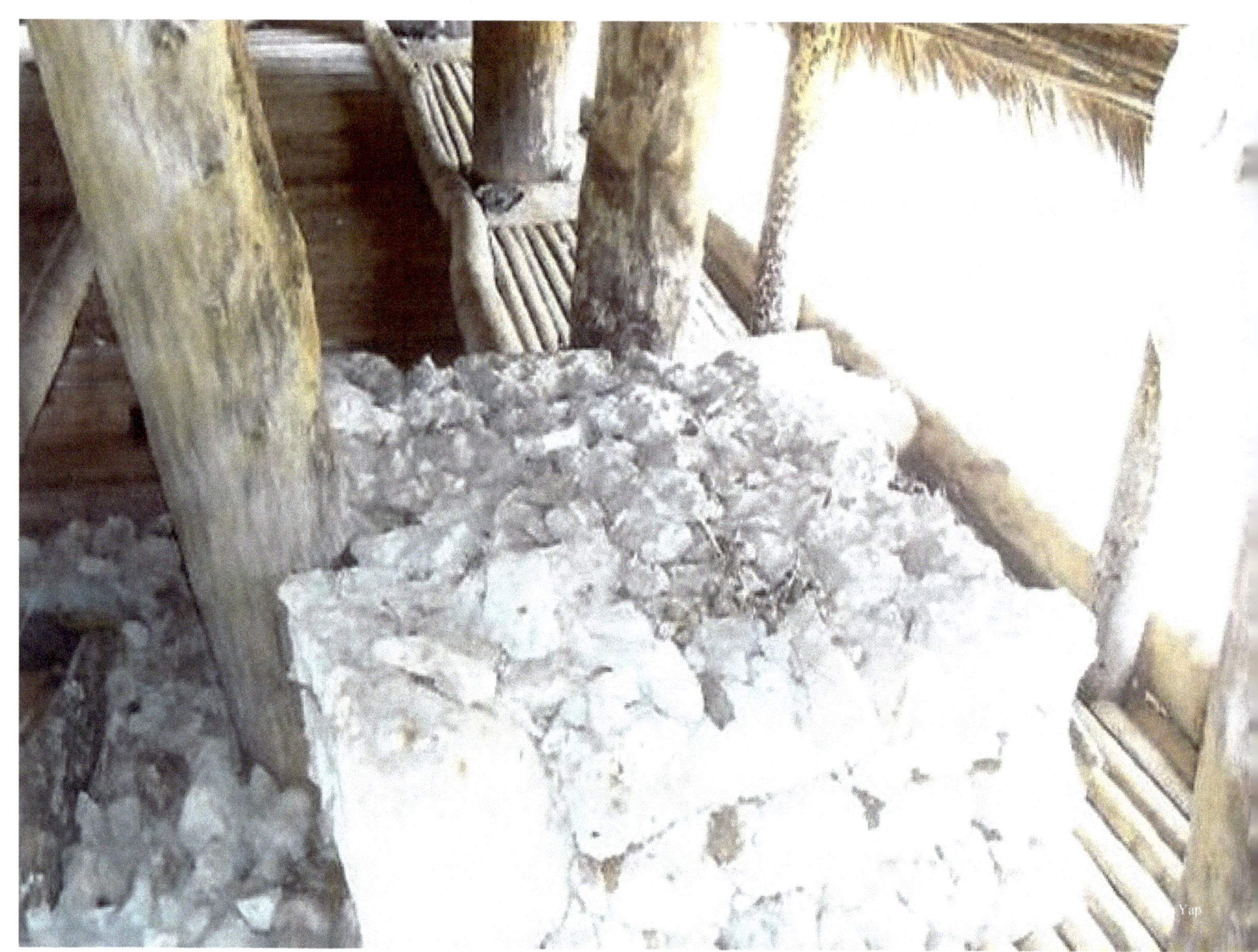
Yap

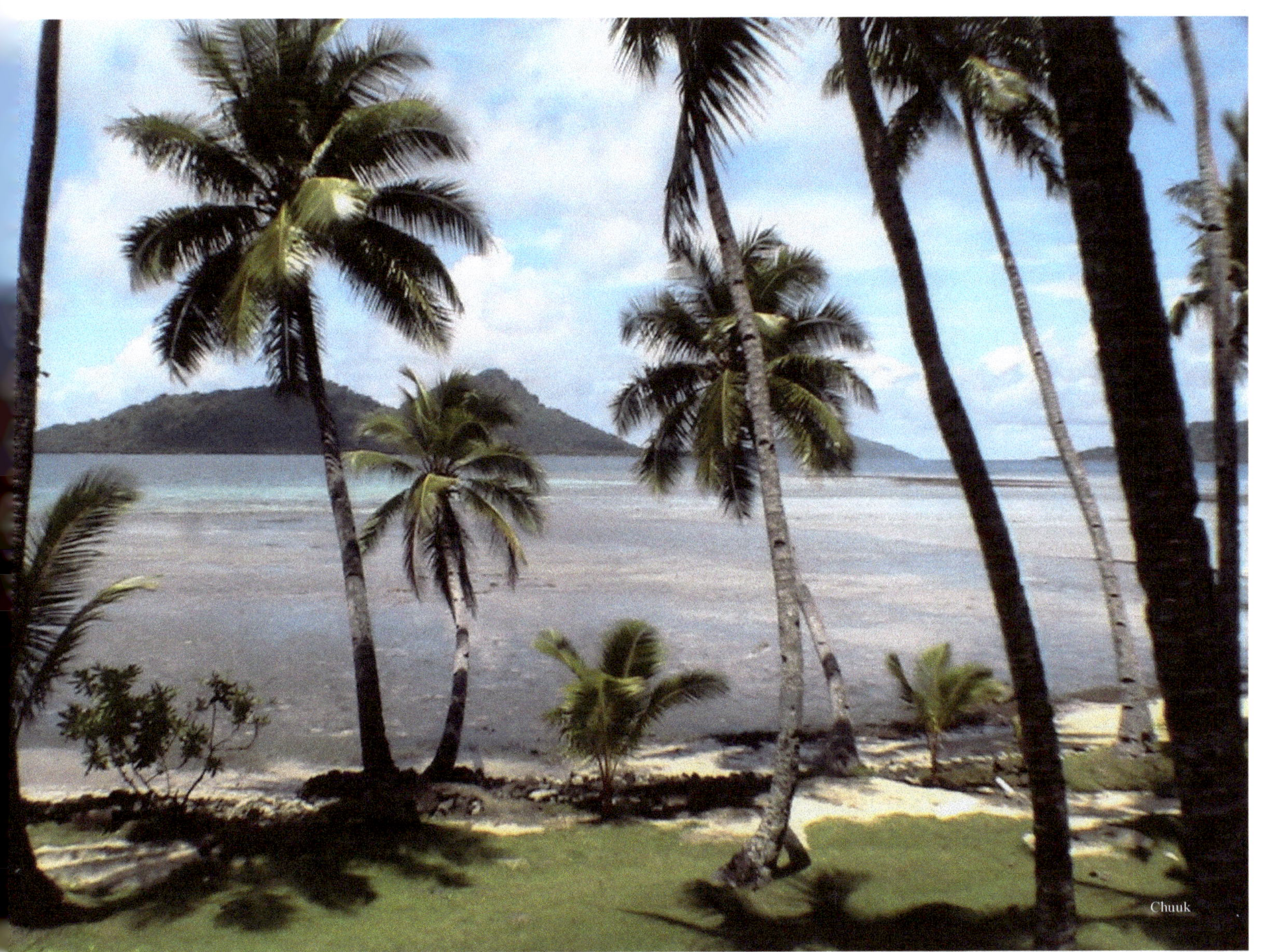

Chuuk

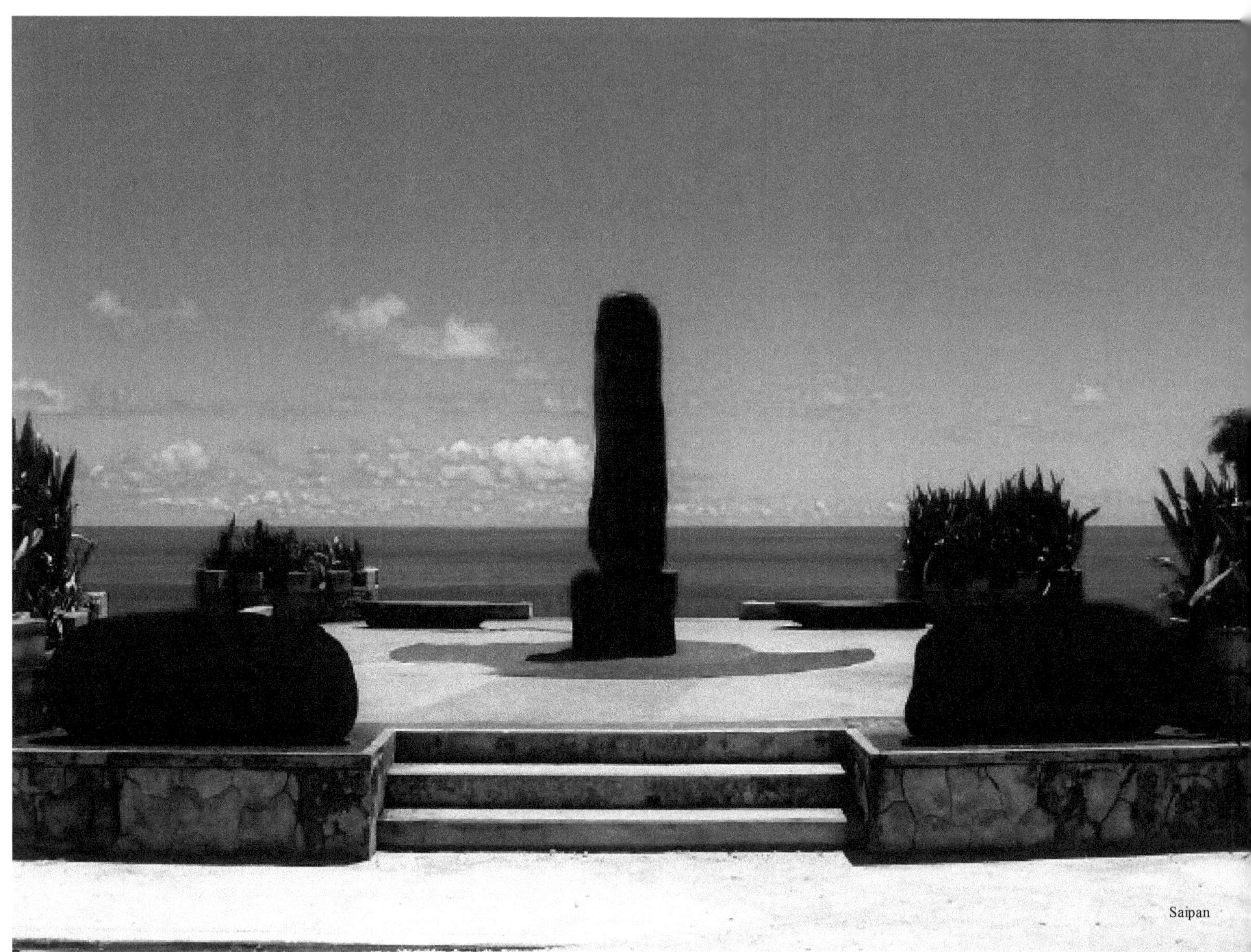

Saipan

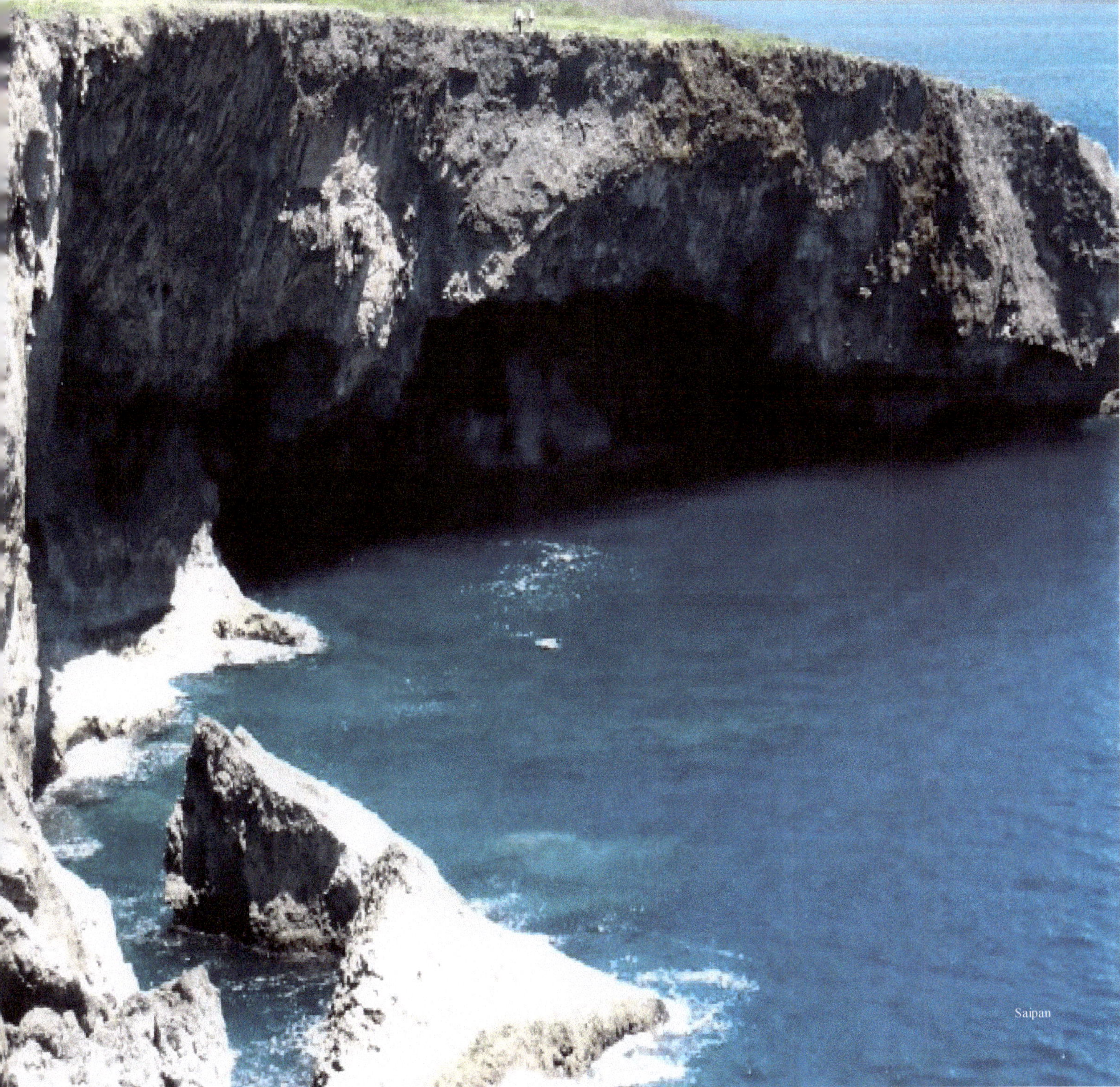
Saipan

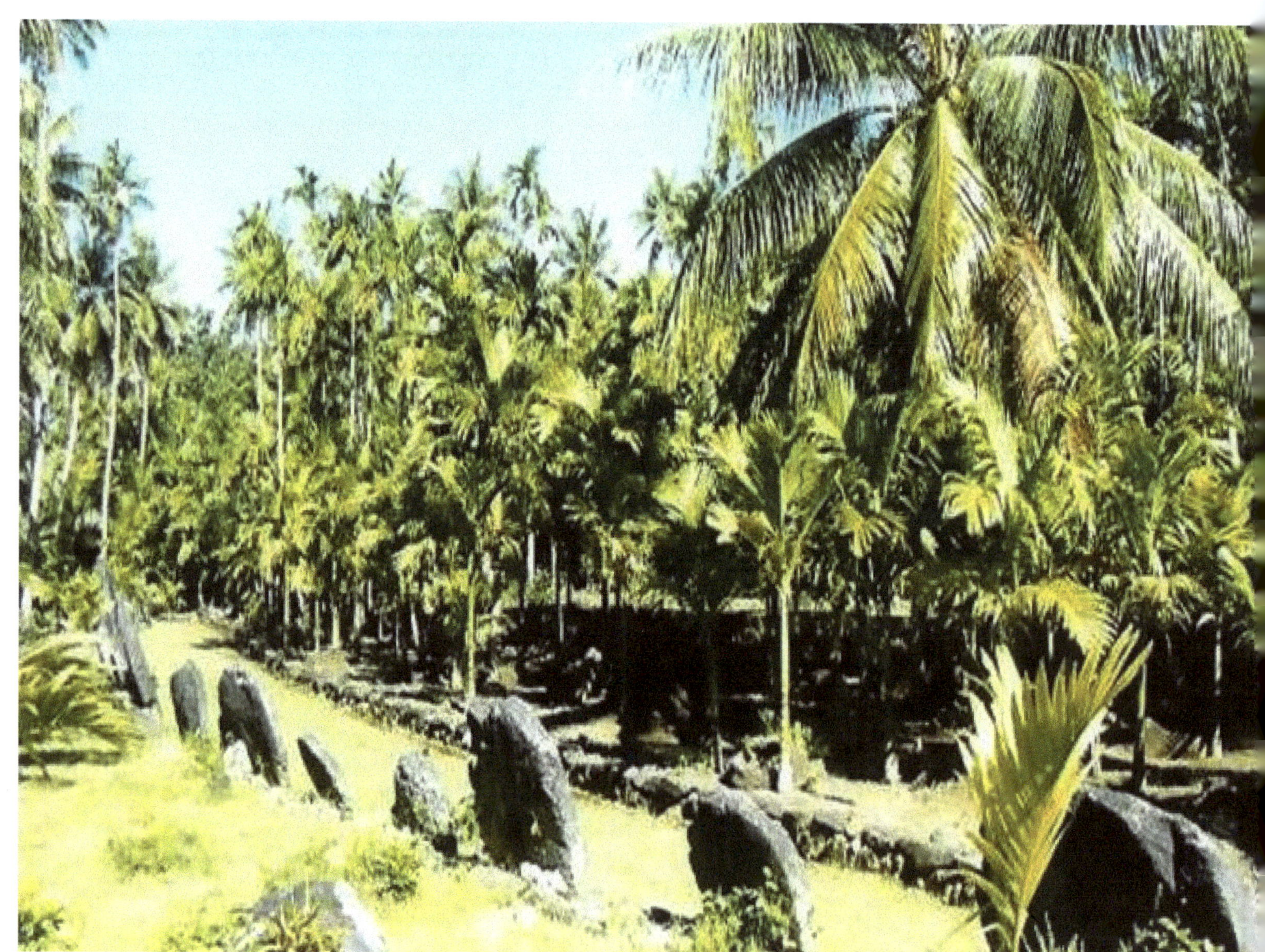

Saipan

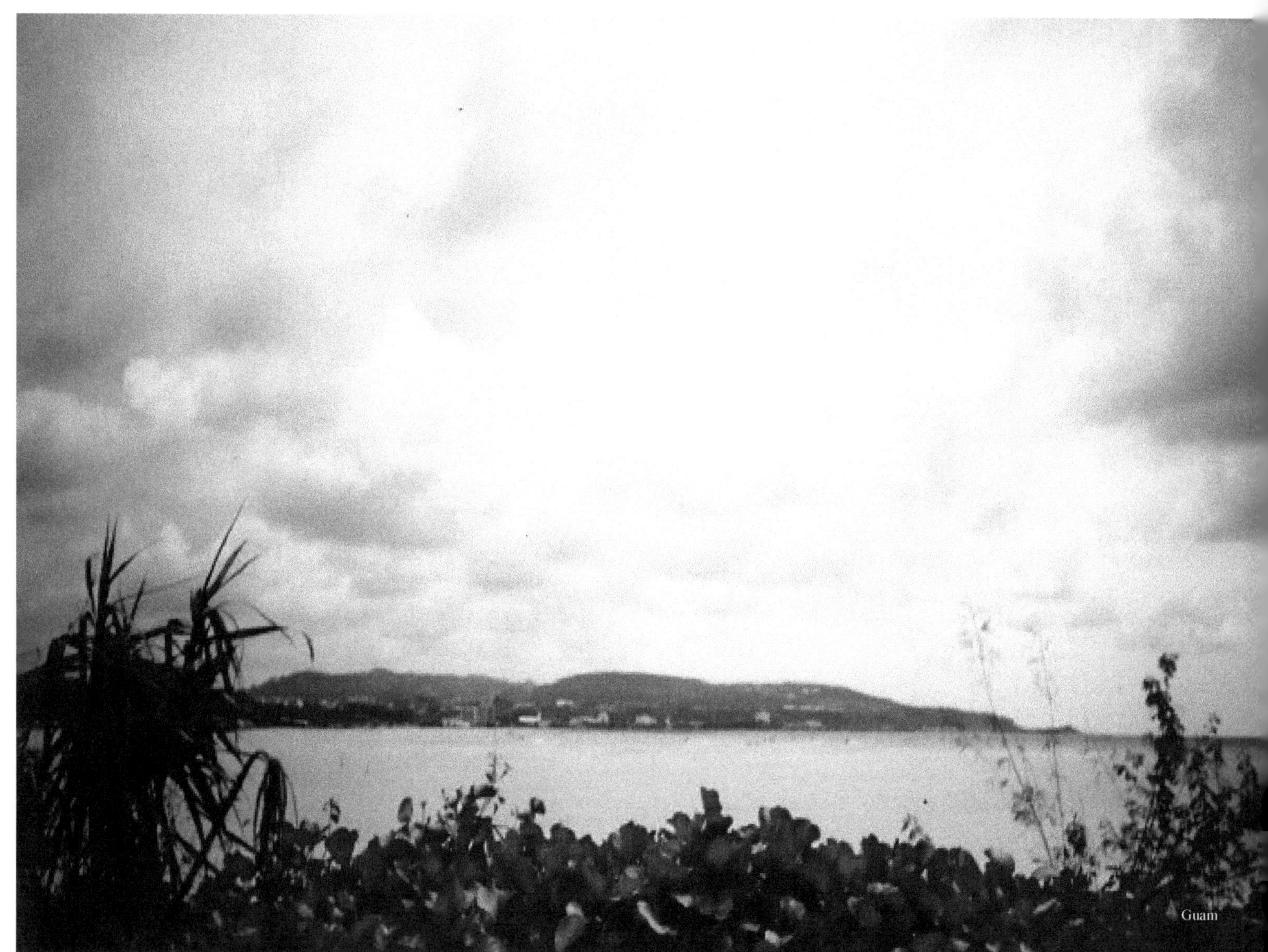

Guam

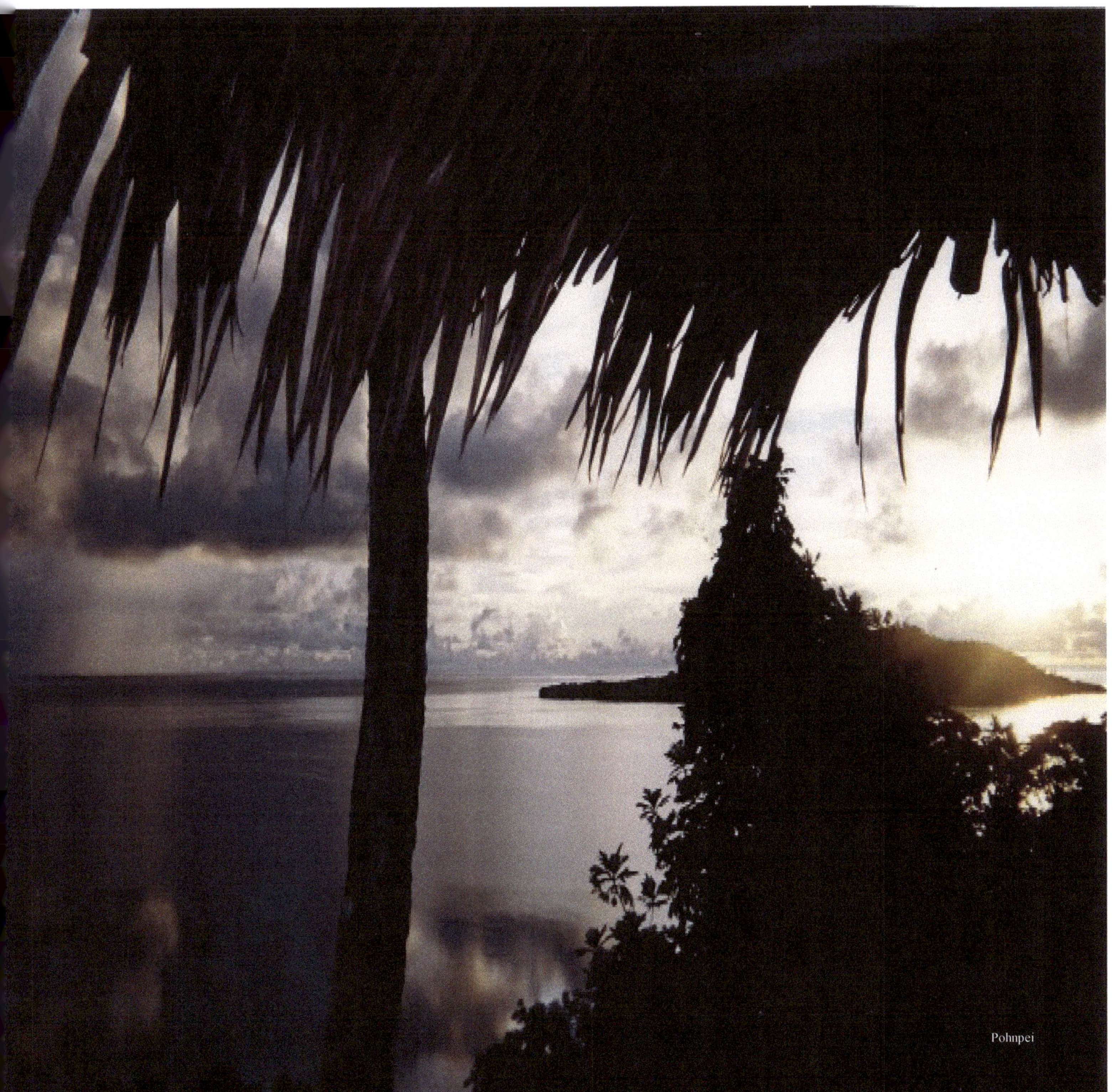

Pohnpei

Other Selected Titles by blue ocean press

Cuba is a State of Mind:

The Spiritual Traveler, Vol I – A Pictorial Journey

p.w. long with Juaquin Santiago & Elijo Truth (2009)

ISBN: 978-4-902837-07-2

Three intrepid travelers who experience and write about the human consciousness of the places they visit, provide a passport into Cuba's cultural, political, spiritual, economic and environmental life. Instead of simply looking at the sights, sounds, and tastes of a locale, the reader is allowed to experience the consciousness of a nation.

This edition uses photographs as the platform on which the essays are experienced by the reader. These allow readers to experience Cuba as a "State of Mind".

Parables of Milk and Might: Development Political Satire -

»The Voices of the Affected«

by RAN (2008)

ISBN: 978-4-902837-21-8

Following over four decades of development politics, after the official end of colonialism in most countries in Africa, South America and Asia, it is difficult for the industrial countries to forgo their economic interests in the developing countries, which are said to be independent. Their continued presence in these countries, controlling, or dictating the trend of economic and political developments, is a proof of the protection of their interests.

Parables of Milk and Might is a satire on the international development sector, in particular, the relationship between the countries of the Global North and South. The book uses a wonderful combination of wordplay, metaphor, and humorous storytelling to get its message across.

From the author:

The main purpose for writing this book is to use it to sensitize many people, both in the industrial countries, as well as in the developing world, particularly in Africa and in Asia, the Caribbean and South American countries, about the negative effects of the global economic system, which is controlled by the powerful and wealthy countries, to the disadvantage of the developing countries. This sensitization will increase the awareness of people about the effects of this negative development, which is the cause of poverty, underdevelopment and conflicts in the world."

Quotes from the book:

 "Mr. Schlotterhose rushes to his friend Prof. Grosskopf for help in the homework of his son, who has to write an essay on a topic in development politics. While both are drinking colonialwater and discussing this topic, three dairy experts, who are professionals on this subject and are preparing to fly to »Ghamaronda« in »Akirfa« come to join them in an impromptu colonialwater party. The dairy experts introduce themselves and give an account of their dairy business in the calveslands…"

This book is translated from its original German.

Green Pearl Odyssey

by Reilly Ridgell (2009)

ISBN: 978- 902837-23-4

The story, set in the mid-1980s, follows a former Peace Corps Volunteer who kills a mobster's son in revenge for the killing of his wife and brother, then runs to the islands of Micronesia to avoid the mobster's hired killers. The culture and geography of the islands become the backdrop for his flight as he tries to stay one step ahead of his pursuers and deal with his own guilt at the same time. The skinny island of Majuro, lush Pohnpei with its mysterious Nan Madol ruins, the isolation of the Mortlocks, the shipwrecks of the Truk Lagoon, the sailing canoes of Polowat and Satawal, the stone money of Yap, and the modernized lifestyle of Guam all have their parts to play as he jumps from island to island. Finally, on Guam, he confronts the mob boss and his own guilt, and tries to resolve both his physical and emotional dilemmas.

The author has written a widely used textbook, *Pacific Nations and Territories*, and is co-author of its elementary level version, *Pacific Neighbors*. He also wrote the anthology *Bending to the Trade Winds, Stories of the Peace Corps Experience in Micronesia*.

What We Bury At Night: Disposable Humanity

by Julian Aguon (2008)

ISBN: 978-4-9028376-76

The fate of Micronesia is the fate of Sustainable Humanity. Micronesia is last domino in the quest to globalize the Earth into a singular monoculture. It is the region least affected by the increasingly global culture of conspicuous consumption and individualistic materialism. Micronesia is at a crossroads, as is the human race. If the last region on earth in which, among the majority of the population, communal living based on interconnectedness, extended families, shared resources, non-linear thinking, and a sustainable relationship with the natural environment is the norm is allowed to be destroyed, the future of humanity is truly in jeopardy. When imagination of indigenous youth and the viability of sustainable living are allowed to die, so does hope for the entire human race. Micronesia is one of the last corners on earth where people, on the whole, still pattern life in humane and interdependent arrangements built on sustaining, life-supporting values, in short, where people still mostly function as people. This resilience, perhaps, is an offering of beauty - its contribution to the world. This book is a series of essays describing the present day realities of the U.S.-Micronesia relationship through the eyes of the folk on the ground, being disappeared. Both elders and youth tell of the continuing harm of the U.S. colonial project in Micronesia, revealing how that project continues to starve the imaginations of entire peoples. Made up of more than 2,000 islands and atolls in three major archipelagos, the Carolines, the Marshalls, and the Marianas, Micronesia was known from the last World War until the 1970s as the Trust Territory of the Pacific Islands. All of it, the Republic of the Marshall Islands (RMI), the Federated States of Micronesia (FSM), the Republic of Palau (Belau), and the Commonwealth of the Northern Mariana Islands (CNMI), less Guam, which was cut from the rest after the Spanish-American war and lumped with the other 1898 Unfortunates: the Philippines, Puerto Rico, and Cuba. While the world looks away, this region of the planet is facing down death. Mostly losing. Current U.S. militarist and corporate plans for the region now threaten to destroy the life-affirming values that bind and sustain these ancient civilizations by deepening dispossession of the people.

How To Rule the World:

Lessons in Conquest by the Modern Prince

by J.F. Cummings (2008)

ISBN: 978-4-902837-00-5

How to Rule the World provides a commentary on today's "modern world" and the "forces" that govern it. This is done in the voice of "civilization's" greatest supporter, an advisor to the Prince. How to Rule the World is a modern adaptation of Machiavelli's The Prince. The author provides the reader, the Prince, with a methodology of non-invasive influence and control that will grant them sovereignty over their desired target nation-state and eventually over the world-at-large.

Learn How To:

- Convince Populations to Participate in Their Own Exploitation

- Use Democracy, Rule of Law, Free Trade, and Free Press As Tools of Domination

- Exploit Cultural & Religious Differences and Use Then to Dominate People

- Promote Anxiety, Insecurity, and Fear As a Means of Social Control

- Use a Nation's Own Culture to Destroy Its Society, Economy, and Environment

- Project Yourself as the Universal Model For Humanity and Civilization

- Create a World Culture of Individualistic Materialism & Perpetual Childhood

- Promote a Culture of Progress At Any Cost

- Convince Nations to Embrace Non-Culture-Based National Planning

How to Rule the World shows the modern Prince how to utilize "modern ideals" such as free trade, democratic governance, human rights, freedom and individual rights, rule of law, and free press to exert control over other nations and convince them to collaborate in their own domination and exploitation through their quest to do whatever is required of them to be accepted as "developed", "modern" nations. Though adherence to the methodology of conquest explained in the book, the Prince will be granted access to the psyche of the target nation's population and will be able to redefine its very sense of worth and self-definition.

Pathway to Change:

A Guide to Personal Transformation

by Martha R. Bireda, Ph.D. (2007)

ISBN: 978-4-902837-47-1

Pathway To Change is a holistic approach to personal transformation that is based upon cognitive behavioral theory and emphasizes cognitive restructuring or belief system change. Participants in the process learn how to identify and modify erroneous and self-defeating beliefs and values that have led to poor choices and negative behaviors in the past. Correctional interventions that include a cognitive skills component have been found to have strong research support for their effectiveness.

Pathway to Change is a cognitive restructuring program that was created to break of cycle of self-destructive thoughts and behaviors in incarcerated populations. It has been implemented in prisons in the US for 10 years and has been highly effectively in reducing the recidivism rates for the inmates who have gone through this process. Ideally participants are taken through Pathway to Change process by a certified PTC facilitator, but over the years we have found that this process is also effective on persons that seriously engage in the process of groups of their own making. This book is both a workbook for participants in a facilitated PTC workshop, as well as a tool for individual personal transformation for anyone who is "stuck".

In addition to its uses for self-therapy and anti-recidivism programs, PTC can also used as very effective tool in Workforce Development, Youth, Personal Empowerment, Employee Placement and Development, Career Counseling, Domestic Violence (for both perpetrators and victims), Substance Abuse, Delinquency Prevention, and Microenterprise/ Entrepreneurship Programs.

Ordering blue ocean press books

Individual Orders:

Books can be purchased and ordered from your local bookstore.

Books can also be purchased online through retailers such as: the Amazon.com family (amazon.com, amazon.co.jp, amazon.co.uk, amazon.fr, amazon.ca, amazon.de), Barnes and Nobles (bn.com, barnesandnobles.com), Powells.com, Abebooks.com, Alibris.com, etc.

Institutional Buyers, Booksellers, and Libraries:

Books can be ordered from the following distributors and wholesalers:

U.S. and Canada:

Ingram Book Group (ipage/Ingram, Ingram Library Services, Ingram International)

Baker & Taylor

NASSCORP (a wholly-owned, for-profit subsidiary of the National Association of College Stores)

U.K. and Rest of World:

Gardners Books

Bertrams

Baker & Taylor

Ingram International